Christopher John Elliott was born in 1943, the son of a watchmaker and a jeweller. He worked as a watch and clock repairer before becoming a Butlins Redcoat. He studied sheet metalwork and set up his own business—he later closed this to concentrate on his love for theatre, creating his own theatre company within a community centre. This theatre is still operating, accommodating various local amateur groups. He has three gorgeous girls from his first marriage and later married Lynne, his rock. He lived in Portugal for seven years before returning to the UK. He managed a community association and several pubs. Wherever he's worked, he has always been involved in entertainment.

Dedicated to Dick Williams.

29th January 1916 – 18th February 2007.

Dick inspired me and taught me all the ingredients required to create theatre. Without him, I would never have been blessed with so many memories—memories that I have passed onto others and will continue to do so.

Christopher John Elliott

CREATING A THEATRE – A STEP BY STEP GUIDE

Transforming a space into a theatre with
no money but determination

AUSTIN MACAULEY PUBLISHERS™

LONDON • CAMBRIDGE • NEW YORK • SHARJAH

A CIP catalogue record for this title is available from the British Library.

The story, experiences, and words are the author's alone.

ISBN 9781398489257 (Paperback)
ISBN 9781398489264 (ePub e-book)

www.austinmacauley.com

First Published 2024
Austin Macauley Publishers Ltd®
1 Canada Square
Canary Wharf
London
E14 5AA

Contents

Introduction

When you see a show in a London theatre, you may think it would be impossible for you to compete with that kind of technology and such professional actors. The people who put these fantastic shows together – including the actors, lighting people, sound people, costume makers and many more – get the same emotional feelings, the same sense of achievement, the same tears in their eyes as the actors, lighting people, sound people, and costume makers in amateur shows in their local halls.

The audience in the London theatre will feel the same emotions as they would feel seeing their Johnny playing the part of 'Oliver' in their local hall.

To be able to put on a show like 'Oliver' in a local hall requires an enormous amount of organisation, but also gives an enormous amount of pleasure.

I was able to do this from nothing, and this book will show how I achieved it and how you could too.

You will need patience, support from others, learn to handle many disappointments, but mainly you will need to have determination.

When you eventually have a theatre environment and are putting on all types of shows, and your organisation can operate financially; then you can expand if you want, or just enjoy all that you have.

How It Happened to Me

Back in 1964, I got a job at Butlins Clacton, not knowing anything about acting or the entertainment industry. During my brief time at Butlins, I fell in love with entertaining people, but because I was a union person and I could see so much favouritism and unfairness, I complained and got the sack.

On returning to London, I joined an amateur drama group with a friend.

After about three years I was in love (and still am) with the theatre environment; especially Old Time Music Hall, because of the variety of theatrical elements, songs, melodramas, sketches, monologues, patter acts, group medleys and plenty more. And so, I decided to form an Old Time Music Hall group.

I still worked with the drama group, while at the same time I developed our new group.

One day, while asking if we could hire an evening at a community centre, the secretary suggested we join the centre as a group on a permanent basis. WE JUMPED AT IT! And from there began the road to a very successful theatre environment, with many stories which will be told throughout this book. (I can't wait to tell you.)

I ran this group for twenty years, and finally got married and moved to Portugal for seven years, leaving the group in capable hands; the theatre environment still exists to this day.

On returning to England, my wife and I ran many pubs; all of which I built stages in and very successfully put on acts. I would have loved to create another theatre situation, but I know how long that can take, and writing this book gives me the opportunity to pass on what I have learnt in my own words, to people wanting to perform or invent.

We now start the nitty gritty; pads at the ready and pencils sharpened.

GOOD LUCK

Early Planning Problems And Structure of Project

If you have no experience, join an amateur drama group that is not a money-making theatrical company (there are plenty of them). Perhaps join a group in an existing theatre, a down-to-earth group where you will learn various skills, or a group that is in a community centre or church where they make their own sets, operate the stage lighting themselves and so on. (Consider this as an apprenticeship as I did.)

You will obviously be expected to join in with everything but whilst in the group and learning various skills, you can increase your knowledge by finding out things you will eventually need to know. This does not have to be a secret from the group or the person running it. The group that I was in encouraged me and we helped each other out in many different ways.

Things to Find Out and Things to Do

1.

Attend local Arts Council meetings (normally in the evenings) to make yourself known. You could always report back to the group you're in about what is being discussed. If possible, always keep in touch with the chairperson and secretary and volunteer if the Arts Council asks; it's a feather in your cap.

2

Just as a matter of future interest, ask the Arts Council secretary if grants are available to amateur drama groups and if there are companies or organisations that help out with new projects, for instance, the Arts Council of Great Britain, Esmee Fairbairn Foundation etc. Use Google. (All the time.)

3

Find out about your new group regarding charitable status and how to apply for grants.

4

Find out about profit or non-profit status regarding your new group. (From the Arts Council secretary.) Don't forget!

5

Find out how you can enter drama festivals. This might be good for your group and credibility.

6

Finances – how much can you charge members of your group? They have to pay for tuition, and the whole group will have to pay subs to use the venue.

7

Ask the Arts Council regarding public liability insurance for what you are doing. AXA is an insurance company that may help.

8

Will you earn from the project and will you finance it with money taken from such as:-

From:-   Tuition Fees
                      Ticket money from shows
                      Grants
                      T-shirt etc
                      Fund raising events

Don't forget, shows cost money to put on. (We will cover this subject as we go on.)

9

DBS check, to be able to teach children.

10

Ask which council department inspects venues to see if it is able to put public shows on.

11

Ask the fire brigade department regarding fire regulations.

12

Although these 12 subjects seem impossible, they are really simple if approached in an organised manner. Once done and documented, it is one hell of a job out of the way, and when it comes to wanting to know about one of them, you will be well in front of the problem.

Finances

Ways of making money to finance this project:

1. Tuition fees.

2. Ticket money from shows.

3. Grants. (already covered)

4. Tee shirts. (also good for publicity)

5. Fund raising events. (covered later)

1.
Tuition Fees

Find out what other groups charge their members for tuition.

Find out their ticket prices for shows, from both local halls and from council theatres.

This will give you an indication of what you could charge.

I believe that the number of students is most important. I would try to keep fees as low as possible so that it encourages people to join, which equals more *bums on seats* and more *publicity*. If your heart is in the project and you can manage to pay your bills, you will have the ideal situation. There will be opportunities that come your way where you will be able to make some extra money, but you must be patient. I'll give you an example of what happened to me.

I have no qualifications regarding theatre or teaching but I am a member of Equity and PRS, and I regard being in the theatre for many years as an apprenticeship, as I previously mentioned. I've met many people within the amateur theatre and professional theatre, and have heard and told many stories. These get passed around and your name may pop up here and there. People come and see your shows and you don't know who they are; some come as parents to see their children in the show, some come because they like theatre. I see shows because I love the theatre and I like to see the way the show is put on. I like to take on the roll as a critic, commenting on the performance, where things could have been done better or spot on (obviously I keep this to myself.) Some people come to see the show because their friend is in it. Any person coming to your show could be a professional director, producer or drama teacher. Their eye will be on technical things, such as the way they went from one scene to the next, or the use of music to enhance a scene, the cuing of the lights, sound, curtains etc. and they will remember that production if it worked.

To come to the point (at last). One day I got a phone call from a lady called Jo Shepherd. (I didn't know then, but she was the mother of Ben Shepherd from Tipping Point.) "Hello, Chris," she said, "I'm Jo Shepherd from Waltham Forest College, and I was wondering if you would run a BETEC course at the college on theatre production?" I was absolutely mad with myself for having no qualifications, I mean, what an opportunity! "I'm really sorry, Jo, I'd love to join you but I have no qualifications." "I know," she said, "but I know what you are capable of."

5

I joined the college, earned good money, put shows together including 'The Matchgirls', book and lyrics by Bill Owen, music by Tony Russel; this will always remain in my memory. Not only was I paid as a tutor, but because of the facilities in our venue, the college asked if I could teach the students there using our lighting and sound systems; for which our venue received payment for using the facilities and hall hire. WHAT A RESULT!

Opportunities Big and Small, Do Come Along.

This also applies to students. During their involvement with this project, they will be introduced to many trades; one of the trades may just catch their attention.

Examples:

My eldest daughter Lucy runs her own very successful theatre academies.

Peter, at 11 years old, was interested in lighting. After many years with us he left college, wired in our stage lighting permanently and now has his own stage lighting company.

Mathew, a teenager with us for several years, became entertainment manager on cruise ships and now runs a holiday camp. His father Brian used to be involved in entertainment, and after helping us he got the enthusiasm to put together a very successful touring tribute band.

Sue, a young girl in her teens, turned up one day and asked if she could be our stage manager. I've never used a stage manager; we usually just get on with it, but I gave her the opportunity and said yes. She was a great asset, and after a couple of years went to college to learn stage management. One day, three years later, she rushed into one of my sessions and said, "I can't stop, but I must say thank you for your help, I'm now a professional stage manager." And she rushed off.

Gary (or Ricky) in Eastenders was a chef in our local pub. He went out with one of my daughters Lucy, and joined our group. After several years he went to drama school and ended up on TV. He'd never acted before.

Zoe joined us while at school and was with us for a very long time. She became production manager for a television company.

These were just a few stories of opportunities, but there are so many trades involved with the theatre that opportunities crop up all the time; far too many to mention but here are some examples:

Acting	Makeup	Publicity
Lighting	Costume design	Printing design
Sound	Costume making	Book keeping
Carpentry	Scenery design	Teaching
Scenery painting	Metal work	Production
Directing	Back stage crew	Electrician
Stage management	Catering	Pyro technics

THE LIST IS ENDLESS

Class Structures

Monday, for ages, 11—18 Youth Training Class. 5 pm to 6.30 pm.
To encourage self and group confidence and stage techniques in preparation for performances.

Monday, for ages, 11—18 Youth Production Class. 6.30 pm to 8 pm.
Students will be involved in plays etc. with the emphasis on total involvement with the presentation and production of shows. Students will be encouraged to attend another class at the centre if entering this session.

Monday, for ages, 16+ Adult Production Class. 8 pm to 10.30 pm.
Music-hall, plays, musicals and panto.

Tuesday, for ages, 11—18 Youth Training Class. 4.30 pm to 6 pm.
As Monday but alternative day.

Tuesday, for ages, 11+ Scenery Design and Manufacture Class. 6 pm to 7 pm.
Students will be involved in the design, building and painting of scenery for forthcoming productions.

Wednesday, for ages, 6—11 Junior Production Class. 4.30 pm to 6 pm.
Students will be involved in plays etc. with emphasis on total involvement with the presentation and production of shows. Before entering this class, students should have some stage knowledge or have attended one of the Junior Training Classes at the centre.

Wednesday, for ages, 11+ Administration Class. 6 pm to 7 pm.
Students will be involved in producing handbills, posters, mailing lists, tickets and the promotion of the theatre project. They will have access to a typewriter, photocopier and computer with expert tuition on operation.

Wednesday, for ages, 11+ Sound Effects and Recording Class. 7 pm to 8 pm.
Students will be taught basic techniques regarding sound cues in relation to the script, lighting and other technical aspects of the theatre. Students will have access to reel-to-reel tape recorders, and will be encouraged to tape their own sound effects for forthcoming productions and operate the equipment of the performance.

Thursday, for ages, 6—11 Junior Training Class. 4.30 pm to 6 pm.
This class aims to encourage young people to work together as a team through drama games, exercises and role playing. You will also be taught various stage techniques, stage terminologies and use of stage equipment.

Friday, for ages, 11+ Stage Lighting Class. 4.30 pm to 6 pm.
This class aims at teaching students basic theatre lighting with the emphasis on students lighting a production themselves. They will be taught cue techniques, plotting of lights and how to operate equipment safely.

Friday, for ages, 6—11 Junior Training Class. 6 pm to 7.30 pm.
As Thursday but alternative day.

Saturday All Ages. Saturday Theatre Club. 10 am to noon.
This is a fun session where students and friends can come to the centre and work out a scene and perform it on stage with full lighting etc. Or, if they would rather, students can join in drama games and exercises. A tuck shop is also available.

The class structure page shows what I aimed at teaching. I asked various tutors to come along and do 'one off' sessions but mainly I taught all the classes. The idea was to introduce students to as many aspects of the theatre as possible. Students should be encouraged to search for themselves either in the library or through Google to gain more information about subjects they are interested in, or just general information on the workings of the theatre. They should be encouraged to tell the rest of the group if they find anything of interest.

One of the main objectives of the classes is to progress from one group to another; and once they are confident enough, they will be involved in full length productions. Obviously, these classes will be in the brochure, advertising what is on offer. The times of classes allows to carry on working and earn a living until such a time as you could, hopefully, do it full time.

I wanted, for a long time, to be involved in the theatre full time. I continually thought of ideas and ways of making it work and was convinced I could do it. The only problem was, I wondered if I will earn enough money. At the time I was working as a consultant for a company earning good money, but had nothing in the bank. The project I was working on came to completion and I was offered the job as works manager. I did this for a year, and because I had made a good job of what I had developed, I was really in surplus and didn't have a lot to do.

Every morning, the Estimator would come into the office, hang up his car jacket and say, "Another boring day." And when he went home in the evening, he would put on his car jacket and say, "Another boring day over." After a year, at Christmas, I opened a Christmas present and guess what, THE SAME CAR JACKET AS THE ESTIMATOR. This made up my mind and I gave in my notice and was out of work (purposely), to try and fulfil my ambition. I had never been out of work before, and to keep up my national insurance etc. I went on the doll (job centre) and as luck would have it, they were running a course on starting your own business. I took on the course and it helped enormously, but then came the hardest decision ever, 'the start date'. This was agreed, I left the job centre and started my theatre project and never looked back. Initially, the tuition fees paid my bills, and then other opportunities turned up; all to do with theatre and made it all more viable.

BROCHURES

I'VE PHOTOCOPIED VARIOUS OLD BROCHURES TO GIVE EXAMPLES OF LAYOUT SUGGESTIONS. THESE ARE ALL BASED ON USING A4 PAPER SIZE. THE BROCHURE BELOW USES 1 SHEET OF A4 AND GIVES 4 PAGES OF INFORMATION;

THIS IS A BROCHURE.

FRONT PAGE (BASIC)

Elliott's Young People's Theatre

presents

YOU'RE ON!

April/May/June

a programme of theatre events, workshops, shows, and fun for young people

You're On!

Monday, 3 April, to Wednesday, 5 April, 10 am to 4 pm

Monday
'Propping' it up – playing scenes with props.

Tuesday
Backstage at 'The Wells' – a visit by coach to one of the most famous theatres in London.

Wednesday
Dressing the part – playing scenes with costumes and props.

Fee £4 a day. Bring lunch or get it here for £1.

Friday, 28 April, 8 pm

Be A Clown!

Gerry Flanagan leads a workshop on clowning improvisation and performance techniques. Come and discover the clown in you! This is the first in a series of workshops leading to a performance later in the year.

Fee for adults £3. For children £1.

Saturday, 6 May, 7.30 pm
Let's do the show right here!

Two evenings of entertainment – scenes, sketches, exercises and surprises by the Young People's Theatre (all classes).
One of the objects of Elliott's YPT is to teach the art of presenting a show – lighting, sound, set, the creation of atmosphere, and the fostering of team spirit. These performances will be entirely by the young people themselves.

Admission for adults £1.50. Admission for children free.

2nd PAGE (BASIC)

Wednesday, 24 May, to Sunday, 28 May, 8 pm
The Dracula Spectacular Show!

Elliott's company get Transylvania mania! You'll be shaking in your seat (with laughter) at the one-man transfusion service and some assorted ghouls – and girls. A combined production by the adult group and the Young People's Theatre.

Tickets £3 concessions £1.50

Tuesday, 30 May, to Friday, 2 June, 10 am to 4 pm
You Can Do It!
We start the week with a visit backstage to the Barbican Theatre, described by the Queen, when she opened it in 1982, as 'one of the wonders of the modern world'. The 109-foot double height 'fly-tower' above the stage is one of the tallest in the world. For the rest of the week, we'll be playing drama games, and doing exercises to build group and individual confidence, putting scenes together (and taking them apart!) leading to a free show for adults on Friday at 2.30 pm.

Fee £4 a day. Bring lunch or get it here for £1.

Friday, 16 June, 8 pm

Be A Clown II!
Meet **Gerry Flanagan** again, and learn some more tricks of the trade.

Fee for adults £3. Fee for children £1.

Friday, 30 June, 8 pm

I Say! I Say! I Say! or 'and now a little song entitled…'
A music-hall workshop with the unflappable Chris Elliott. Getting on, staying on, and getting off; putting over a song or a joke; how to relax and enjoy yourself in front of an audience, and how to make sure they enjoy you.

Fee for adults £3. Fee for children £1.

BACK PAGE (BASIC)

We also offer the following specialist classes:

Speech Training for Young People
Tutor: Joy Gailer LGSM. (Member of the Society of Teachers of Special Drama, and the English-Speaking Board.)
Fridays 4.30 pm to 6 pm in the Green Room. Please ask for details.

Effective Speaking for the Businessman
Tutor: Roy Seanunen LGSM GODA. (Examiner in Speech and Public Speaking for the Guildhall School of Music and Drama.)
Group day courses arranged. Please ask for details.

Drama Workshops for Schools
Tutor: Chris Elliott. Equity member.
Workshops can be provided at the school or our centre. Transport to the centre can be arranged in certain circumstances. Please ask for details.

We believe that people of all ages, and from all walks of life, can benefit from knowledge of the theatre, and that its techniques can be applied in everyday life to build self-awareness and self-confidence in everyone, from the school child to the company director. This is our message – and our aim.

Events and classes all take place at the Forest Community Association Centre, Guildford Road, (off Hale End Road, next to Wadham Bridge) Waltham stow E17.
For information and bookings, please write or phone Chris Elliott at 24 Abbotts Crescent, Highams Park E4 9SA Telephone 5311360.

BROCHURES

THE BROCHURE BELOW USES 1 SHEET OF A4 AND GIVES 4 PAGES OF INFORMATION BUT WHEN OPENED WE USE A HINGE DESIGN (PUT THE TWO PAGES TOGETHER AND SEE WHAT I MEAN)

FRONTPAGE HINGE

Elliott's Young People's Theatre

presents

Theatre FUN

An exciting programme of Theatrical events

Visit a West End Theatre by coach.

Put on your own show each week for family and friends.

Operate stage lights with professional tuition.

Record your own sound effects with tuition.

Dress up in stage costumes.

1st WEEK. 30th July – 3rd August.

STAGE EFFECTS WEEK

£3 per day or £12 for the week.

2nd WEEK. 6th August – 10th August.

GET MESSY WEEK

£3 per day or £12 for the week.

3rd WEEK. 13th August – 17th August.

"ROYAL OPERA HOUSE"

At Elliott's Young People's Theatre ALL WEEK

4th WEEK. 20th August – 24th August.

"MARCEL MARCEAU" MIME WEEK

£3 per day. (Thursday £8) or £17 for the week
which includes back stage visit, coach and show.

5th WEEK. 28th August – 31st August.(starts Tuesday)

SHOW WEEK

£3 per day or £10 for the week.

ALL DAYS ARE FROM 10am–4pm
BRING PACKED LUNCH.

BANGS ! SMOKE ! PUFFS ! DRY ICE ! SNOW !
LIGHTNING ! STRANGE NOISES ! (Plus lots of Fun).
Learn about them all!!! Use these effects in your own
show on the Friday and show your friends.

Learn how to make Stage Props and use them on Friday
in your own show.

Theatrical Fun throughout the week

A very special week of Dance with two dancers
one musician and a set designer all from The
'ROYAL OPERA HOUSE' Covent Garden.

Limited places. Please book in advance. £15 for the week.

Part of this week we study MIME TECHNIQUE. Then on
Thursday we go BACKSTAGE at The 'Sadler's Wells Theatre'.
Have your lunch and then see The Worlds leading Mime
'Marcel Marceau' in his own show. Return about 6pm.

This week we DRESS UP IN STAGE COSTUMES.

We end the week with a 'GRAND FINALE' show for
your friends to come and see.

TUCK SHOP WILL BE OPEN FOR:--
Drinks, Sweets and Crisps.

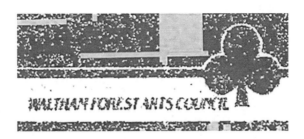

Dramas workshops for schools

Tutor: Chris Elliott, Equity member

Workshop can be provided at the school or our centre transport to the centre can be arranged in certain circumstanced. Please ask for details.

Saturday 10 am to 12 noon

Saturday Theatre club

This is a fun session where students and friends can come to the centre and work out a scene and perform it on stage with full lightning etc. Or, if they would rather, students can join in drama and exercise. A tuck shop is also available!

We believe that people of all ages, and from all walks of life, can benefit from knowledge of the theatre, and that is techniques can be applied in everyday life to build self-awareness and self confidence in everyone, from the school child to company director. This is our message; and our aim.

Events and classes all take place at the Forests community association centre Guilford Road, coff hale end road, next to Wadham bridge, Waltham stow E17.

For information and bookings please write or phone **Chris Elliott.**

24 Abbotts Crescent, Highams Park, E4 9SA, Telephone 531 1360

THE BROCHURE BELOW USES 2 SHEETS OF A4 AND IS STAPLED TOGETHER TO MAKE A BOOKLET
GIVING 8 PAGES OF INFORMATION

FRONT PAGE STAPLES

ELLIOTT'S
Young People's Theatre

presents

You're On!

*a programme of theatrical classes,
workshops, shows and fun for young
people*

Elliott's Young People's Theatre

Elliott's Young People's Theatre based at the Forest Community Centre in Walthamstow gives youngsters from 6-18 years the chance to take part in all aspects of the theatre. Whether you're interested in performing, designing scenery and costumes or learning more about what happens backstage with lighting, sound and even administration Elliott's Young People's Theatre is the place to find out.

Classes and workshops are run by professional actors and people with vast theatrical experience. This year Elliott's Young People's Theatre welcomes the expertise of Phillip Chard who joins the Centre from The Phantom of the Opera where he was stage manager.

Also Lindsey Coulson from BBC1's 'A Bear Behind' will be offering advice and teaching workshops on various theatre skills.

A full programme of events including classes, workshops, shows and visits is listed here but if you have any further queries please don't hesitate to call in or phone.

Regular Classes at the Centre

Monday

5pm.-6.30pm. 11-18 years
Youth Training Class

To encourage self and group confidence and stage techniques in preparation for performance

Monday

6.30pm.-8pm. 11-18 years
Youth Production Class

Students will be involved in plays etc. with the emphasis on total involvement with the presentation and production of shows. Students will be encouraged to attend another class at the Centre if entering this session.

Monday

8pm.-10.30pm. 16+
Adult Production Class

Music-hall, plays, musicals and panto

Tuesday

4.30pm.-6pm. 11-18 years
Youth Training Class

As Monday but alternative day

Tuesday

6pm.-7pm. 11+
Scenery Design and Manufacture Class

Students will be involved in the design building and painting of scenery for forthcoming productions.

Wednesday

4.30pm.-6pm. 6-11 years
Junior Production Class

Students will be involved in plays etc. with the emphasis on total involvement with the presentation and production of shows. Before entering this class students should have some stage knowledge or have attended one of the Junior Training Classes at the Centre.

Wednesday

6pm.-7pm. 11+
Administration Class

Students will be involved in producing handbills, posters, mailing lists, tickets and the promotion of the Theatre project. They will have access to a typewriter, photocopier and computer with expert tuition on operation.

Wednesday

7pm.-8pm. 11+
Sound Effects and Recording Class

Students will be taught basic techniques regarding sound cues in relation to the script, lighting and other technical aspects of the theatre. Students will have access to reel to reel tape recorders and will be encouraged to tape their own sound effects for forthcoming productions and operate the equipment at the performance.

Thursday

4.30pm.-6pm. 6-11 years
Junior Training Class

This class aims to encourage young people to work together as a team through drama games, exercises and role playing. You will also be taught various stage techniques, stage terminology and use of stage equipment.

Friday

4.30pm.-6pm. 11+
Stage Lighting Class

This class aims at teaching students basic theatre lighting with the emphasis on students lighting a production themselves. They will be taught cue techniques, plotting of lights and how to operate equipment safely.

Friday

6pm.-7.30pm. 6-11 years
Junior Training Class

As Thursday but alternative day

Saturday

10am.-12 noon All ages
Saturday Theatre Club

This is a fun session where students and friends can come to the Centre and work out a scene and perform it on stage with full lighting etc. Or, if they would rather, students can join in drama games and exercises. A tuck shop is also available!

Theatrical Events

January

Monday 1 - Wednesday 3
10am.-4pm.
Tabs, Spots and Other Things!

Everyone working in or interested in the theatre should know something about backstage work. This workshop concentrates on stage lighting, sound and curtains, showing how they can make or ruin a performance.
Fee £4 per day. Bring a packed lunch or buy one here for £1

February

Saturday 3
8pm.

Members of The Young People's Theatre will perform their entry for The Waltham Forest Drama Festival.
Tickets adult £2
(under 16's / OAP £1.50)
Bar opens 7.30pm.

Monday 19 - Friday 23
10am.-4pm.
National Theatre Workshop Week.

Take a coach trip to the South Bank for a look around the National Theatre, one of the most modern and technically advanced in the world. This will be followed up on Friday by the National Theatre visiting Elliott's Young People's Theatre to hold a workshop on improvisation techniques. During the week you will find out about drama festivals - how they work, what you need to enter one and have the chance to perform your own scenes and adjudicate them.
Fee £4 per day. Bring a packed lunch or buy one here for £1

March

Saturday 10 - Sunday 11
10am.-4pm.
Dance Drama Weekend

An exciting weekend of Dance Drama with professional tuition ending on Sunday with a show for parents and friends.
Fee £4 per day. Bring a packed lunch or buy one here for £1.

April

Monday 9 - Friday 13
10am.-4pm.
Technical Theatre Workshop

This week will cover make-up techniques, sound effects, lighting, recording and many other aspects of technical theatre. There will also be a backstage visit to the Sadlers Wells Theatre, original site of a theatre since 1683 and now home to

both the Sadlers Wells Ballet Company and the new Sadlers Wells Opera Company.
Fee £4 per day. Bring a packed lunch or buy one here for £1.

Saturday 14
Odd Socks Theatre
Company

A fun workshop and short show for all the family with local professional company Odd Socks.
Doors and bar open 7.30pm.
Show starts 8pm.
Tickets £2 (under 16's £1.50)

Monday 16 - Friday 20
10am.-4pm.
Stage Technique
Workshop

The week will include a backstage tour of The Royal Festival Hall and a follow up visit by Wayne Pritchett, professional mime artist best known for his BBC Series 'Body Talk'. He will give tuition on movement for the forthcoming production of Grease. The week will also include singing, mime and production techniques associated with performance.
Fee £4 per day. Bring a packed lunch or buy one here for £1.

May

Saturday 5 - Sunday 6
10am.-4pm.
Mask Weekend

Fun weekend on how to make masks and act with them. Finish off with a short show for friends using the masks you've made.
Fee £4 per day. Bring a packed lunch or buy one here for £1.

Monday 28 - Friday June 1
10am.-4pm.
Clown Workshop

A week of fun and mess! The workshops will include all you need to know about pie-in-the-face routines and general slapstick.
During the week there will be a visit to the Westminster Theatre which in 1982 earned the distinction of being the only London theatre to stage a play written by a Pope - "The Jewellers Shop" by John Paul II.
Also included will be a visit by Gerry Flanagan, international clown, who will teach various clowning skills. Round the week off with a performance for friends and parents, full of custard pies and laughter.

June

Monday 18 - Saturday 23

Elliotts Young People's
Theatre present "Grease"

If you would like to audition or be involved in this production in any way contact Chris Elliott on 531-1360 before February 1990.
Also make a note in your diary to come and see the show!

Summer Holiday Specials

From Tuesday July 24th - six weeks of exciting workshops and visits to make the long school holidays fun.

Events will include coach trips, stage fighting workshops, practical sessions on lighting, make up, scenery design and much more. These workshops are very popular so book early.

Full details from Chris Elliott on 531-1360.

Fees

The fees for all activities may be waived in certain circumstances. Please ask for details as early as possible.

Numbers

Numbers are limited at some of these events so you are advised to book early wherever possible.

Tutors

Tutors for The Young People's Theatre include

Alistair Roberts BA
Don Munro, Professional Director
Chris Elliott, Professional Actor
Dave Millard LLAM, Director of Millipede Theatre Group
Phillip Chard, Professional Stage Manager

BROCHURES

BACK PAGE STAPLES

How to Find Us

Events and classes take place at the Forest Community Centre, Guildford Road, Walthamstow E17 (temporary access due to road works via juntion of Hale End Road and the North Circular)
Tel: 527-3810 *24 hour ansaphone*

Elliott's Young People's Theatre

Elliott's Young People's Theatre run various other events and shows throughout the year. If you would like to be involved with the group or would like to be put on the mailing list please complete the slip below and return to Chris Elliott *(address below)*

Information and Bookings

For information or bookings please contact the Centre or Chris Elliott, 24 Abbotts Crescent, Highams Park, E4 9SA. Tel: 531-1360

Please tick the areas you would like to be involved in

☐ Front of house staff

Practical skills i.e:

☐ set building, maintenance

☐ poster/leaflet distribution

☐ transport

any other _____

Tick here ☐ if you would like to be put on the mailing list.

Name _____

Address _____

_____

Telephone No: _____

The sketch below shows an A4 sheet that is folded twice and gives us a front page, *A* back page and 4 pages for more information.

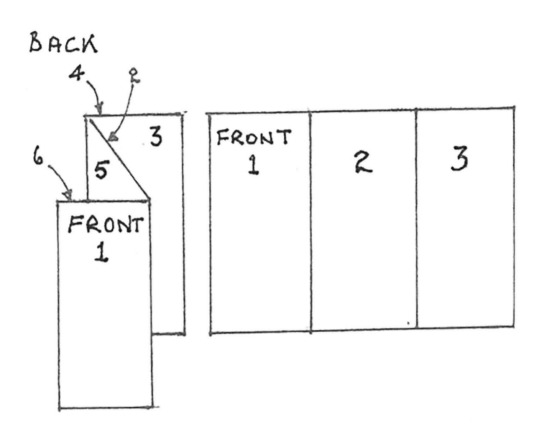

Schools – Council

Special Note: Instead of Calling Our Premises 'Venue', Call It 'Centre'

We are focusing on young people in schools; we believe this project will give them a chance to get involved in an activity that has so many things to get involved in, and also has an end product, a show. During this process, they will learn many skills – too many to mention here – but will be taught as they proceed throughout the project.

Schools are our main source of members and obviously our main source of income, but more importantly, our main source of *publicity*. If you can create a relationship with local schools, you will be reaching out to thousands of people that will have an opportunity to get involved in a new project; whether it's seeing a show, a theme evening, helping within the project or just watching their children develop in so many ways.

A brochure taken home by one school child will reach mum, dad, brother, sister, grandad, grandmother, uncle, aunt. These are just eight people. Each of these people have contact with at least one other person, which now equals 16 people. Let's say an average class has 20 children, this means every 20 children could reach 320 people. If we say an average school has 140 children (this is a very small number!) this will equal 140 divided by 20 = 7 classes $7 \times 320 = 2240$ or 140 pupils $\times$ 16 contacts = 2240 potential receivers of your publicity per school. This will not only advertise your classes, but all your shows and special events. You must be well organised and have very good-quality tuition and shows etc., as near to professional standards as possible.

You need to have the edge on other groups

Offer 'special events' to catch the eye of teachers and head teachers, for example:

Basic brochure 1st page.
Hire a double decker bus or coach and arrange a backstage visit to the Sadler's Wells Theatre, one of the most famous theatres in London. Learn about the 'Ghost of Sadler's'.

Basic brochure back page.
Drama workshops for schools. At your school or at our centre. Transport can be arranged.

Brochure hinge 1st and 2nd pages.
Two dancers to visit the centre from the Royal Opera House. Plus, a musician and a set designer from Covent Garden. A workshop for dance and set design.

Brochure staples 4th page.
Drama festival. We enter our play into the local drama festival.

Brochure staples 4th page.
Back stage visits by coach to the national theatre, one of the world's most modern and technically advanced theatres in the world.

Brochure staples 4th page.
The national theatre visits our centre. Teaching improvisation and other theatrical techniques.

Brochure staples 5th page.
A fun workshop and short show, for all family with local professional company 'odd socks'.

Brochure staples 5th page.
Visit the royal festival hall by coach, and a follow up visit at our centre by professional mime artist, Wayne Pritchet, with a workshop on mime techniques.

Brochure staples 5th page.
Visit Westminster Theatre by coach, followed by a visit from, Gerry Flanagan, international clown who will teach various 'clowning techniques' at the centre.

INTERESTING POINTS FROM THE BROCHURES.

Boarding a coach to London and going back stage at a theatre is very exciting and special. Not many people have the opportunity to see the workings of a theatre or a ghost at Sadler's Wells.

The national theatre like a double decker bus that can be lifted the same as scenery and lowered beneath the stage. This is achieved by an enormous *drum* which is FIVE STORIES HIGH!

PROFESSIONALS THAT HAVE BEEN TO OUR CENTRE.

Royal Opera House
The National Theatre
Odd socks
Wayne Pritchet
Gerry Flanagan
Paul Daniels (I'll tell you about this later)

WHEN THESE EVENTS HAPPEN ASK THE LOCAL PAPER TO ATTEND. FOR PUBLICITY!

We also had ITV come down and film various exerts from a full-length musical that we wrote, and it was shown on the 6 o'clock news three time in one week. PUBLICITY!

Our next job is to give the project/theatre a name and if possible, maybe a logo representing the project/theatre.

Regarding the name of the theatre, I used my own name and called it 'Elliott's Young Peoples Theatre' for the younger people.

'Elliot's Music Hall Company' is our adult group for music hall and musicals.

For plays (adult group) 'Wadham Players' because the centre was next to Wadham Bridge.

You need to work out your own name.

Other groups in our area used for instance;

CADOS	(Chingford Amateur Dramatic & Operatic Society)
DRAMA E4	(because of their postcode)
WOODFORD PLAYERS	because of their area.

You need to produce a basic brochure. No need for council logos yet. This basic brochure is to enable you to go to schools to see their response. Your next step is to go to the Arts Council and get their response; if the responses are favourable, you'll need to produce a proper brochure that you can hand out to everyone. No logos yet, see the Arts Council and Main Council for logos, after you are established.

THIS BROCHURE MUST HAVE:

1.

Your aim. See back page of HINGE BROCHURE. 'We believe PUT ONTO BACK PAGE of all your brochures.

2.

On the front page of all your young people's brochures, always put 'A programme of theatrical classes, workshops, shows and fun for young people'.

3.

Contact details

Your name
Phone number
Address
E mail etc etc……

Put on the back page of your brochure.

YOU NOW NEED THE LIST OF CLASSES AND POSSIBLE SPECIAL EVENTS SIMILAR TO THE STAPLE BROCHURE

I think you should produce a brochure similar to the staple brochure using 2 A4 sheets of paper to get people's interest. This can always be adjusted at a later date. The 1st brochure is just a sample of what you are intending to do.

There is no point in doing three classes a week, the project will go nowhere.

If you are enthusiastic, ambitious and determined go for it!

Always talk to people for comments and support.

FINALLY.

You must have in this your 1st Important Brochure: 'We offer as an introduction a free full or half-day workshop at your school'. Also mention to the head/teacher that you are showing your brochure so that you are able to put on a show for the PTA (parent teachers association) for a very reasonable price.

I would strongly recommend an Old Time Music Hall with the chairman and piano with all the various acts that are available.

Songs
Melodrama
Sketches
Jokes
Group medleys
Monologues

These should be performed in the correct period, before 1914. Not only is this very popular, but it is a fantastic exercise for actors and singers, both young and old. When I was running the theatre, we always put on a performance in the Music Hall and at one point, we were doing a regular show every Sunday night, which became like a club; with waiters, waitresses and a bar. This is a big money-maker regarding private functions in halls and all types of venues. As long as it is in period and performed seriously, it could be a very profitable venture. If you have a permanent class doing Music Hall, you will have no problem finding material to use regarding songs.

Venue

On page 31 there is a drawing of a typical hall with a stage etc., and a list of possible requirements to be able to produce a show for an audience. Let's look at each feature.

1. AUDITORIUM. This must be able to seat enough audience to be profitable, let's say 100 seats, to enable you to put a show on, and be available for the show to run for several evenings. You need to work out your total expenses and do the calculation.

2. AUDIENCE CHAIRS AND TABLES. Has the hall got storage space for chairs and tables?

3. KITCHEN. Is the size of the kitchen okay? And could it be enhanced.

4. TOILETS. Are they adequate?

5. STAGE. If there is no stage, is there room for one.

6. WINGS. Are they adequate?

7. ACCESS BEHIND THE STAGE. If there is no way of getting to the other side of the stage, would it be possible to hang a curtain next to the back wall of the stage to create a passage?

8. FRONT CURTAIN TRACK (FOR CURTAINS). If there isn't one, can one be installed?

9. PROSCENIUM ARCH. If no there is no arch, can one be created with curtains?

10. HEIGHT ABOVE STAGE (RE LIGHTING) If no lights are available, would it be possible to put some up?

11. LIGHTING BOX. If there is no lighting box, is there a room at the end of the hall to put the lighting and sound equipment? In the centre where I worked, there was no lighting box or room, so I personally built a Mezzanine floor above the bar and extended it across the width of the hall. (As drawing shows above 17 and 11.)

12. ROOMS FOR CLASSES. It's important to have at least one room. Maybe use the green room.

13. STORAGE ROOMS WITHIN THE CENTRE. If no storage areas see next item.

14. POSSIBLE AREA FOR CONTAINER STORAGE. The centre where I worked, was had limited storage space, but outside the building I was able to put 3 forty-foot containers. One for scenery, one for props and one for wardrobe.

15. CAR PARKING. Is it adequate? If not, can cars park on the road?

16. FIRE EXIT DOORS. Are they adequate and legal? Check with authorities.

17. DRINKS BAR. Does it have a bar? Is the venue licensed for alcohol? If not, it can be applied for.

18. AUDITORIUM. Ensure the ceiling height and structure can support stage lighting.

GREEN ROOM. Is there a room behind the stage for dressing and access to the stage.

APRON. Under the apron is a good storage space. Worth looking at.

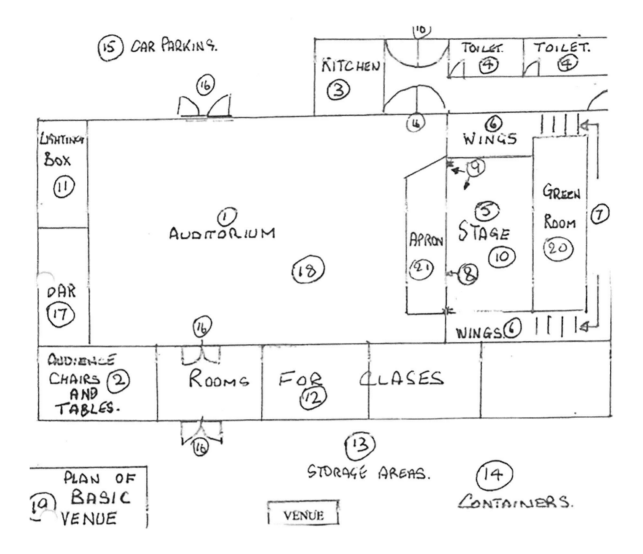

DESCRIPTION OF NUMBERS

1. Audience seating. (Auditorium.)
2. Audience chairs.
3. Kitchen (interval).
4. Toilets. (Audience and actors etc.)
5. Stage.
6. Wings.
7. Access behind stage.
8. Front curtain track (curtain rail).
9. Proscenium arch.
10. Height above stage. (re lights etc.)
11. Lighting box.
12. Rooms for classes.
13. Storage areas within venues bound area.
14. Possible area for container storage.
15. Car parking.
16. Fire exit doors.
17. Drinks bar.
18. Auditorium. (Ceiling height for lighting, fixings etc.)
19. This is a plan of a basic venue for us to discuss.
20. Green room.

VENUE

Finding a venue can be a long process and is a matter of elimination.

Let's look at the type of buildings that would accommodate a theatre.

A large empty building.

Community centre.

A barn.

An old theatre. Empty. With a preservation order on it.

Existing theatre. Council-run.

Church hall.

Village hall.

Farm building.

An existing group needing help.

Whoever you approach, explain that the theatre will bring many people to it and hopefully make it profitable. We looked at special events such as 'London Theatres', professional people coming to give workshops at the centre etc., but we also need to look at special events to encourage adult participation. I've already mentioned 'Old Time Music Hall' which I believe could be a main attraction, but let's look at a few more and list them.

THE ITEMS BELOW WILL OBVIOUSLY NOT TAKE PLACE
UNTIL THE GROUP IS WELL ESTABLISHED.

Old time music hall

Medieval banquets

Seafood evenings

Quiz nights   Various themes

Murder dinners

Feature nights   Fawlty towers

Tribute bands and   Solo singers

Hog roasts   And many more   (and of course pantomimes)

All of the above, except Panto, will have food and drinks. Also, possibly, transport at a cost; maybe through a deal with cab companies.

THIS WHOLE PROJECT IS A 'THEATRICAL EXPERIENCE'

LET'S DEAL WITH THE VENUES.

A large empty building	Although this would be ideal, it would require heavy investment and backing with a lot of financial support. There may be people interested to back it.
Community centre	This is more viable proposition as a new input for the community centre, which will generate income and provide another facility for the local community.
A barn	Again, this will require investment.
An old empty theatre	This will require investment.
Existing council theatre	Possibly a good idea but may have many restrictions.
Church hall	Worth looking into.
Village hall	Good idea, but be careful to secure your involvement. They may think THEY can do it! Once you have done all the hard work. (I'll tell you a story in a minute.)
Farm building	Worth looking into.
An existing group	They may welcome you with open arms, worth looking into.

My Short Story

At the beginning of this book, I mentioned 'how it happened' and told how my wife and I ran several pubs. This was after an annoying experience which I had.

After returning from Portugal, we were not sure what to do, although I would have loved to go back into theatre, but it would have taken ages. We visited a friend of ours, a publican, who ran our local pub. He kindly offered us the use of his cottage for a few months but then came along another friend, who also was a publican and asked if we wanted to run his pub, which seemed like an interesting offer and so we moved in. Our friend wanted to go to Portugal to see if he could find a bar to buy; he visited us several times while we were in Portugal and fell in love with the area. He trained us up which allowed him to go to Portugal for a while. Eventually, we bought a house on Canvey Island and once we settled in, I started thinking about theatre ideas. One day Lynne said (several times), "You'll have to get a job!" I picked up the local paper, and in the job section I phoned the first vacancy. And in the morning, I started working in a company putting magazines into cellophane envelopes.

As days went by, I browsed job vacancies and found a vacancy for a senior bar person. Off went my CV, and after a week I was asked to go for an interview; the job was in a community centre. A week later, I received a phone call from the community centre chairperson and she said, "We've got some good news and some bad news, what would you like to hear first?" I replied the bad news first and she said, "The bad news is, you haven't got the job as senior bar person. The good news is would you be our Community Centre Manager!" This was due to my CV, and I went for a discussion with the committee. I asked what they wanted me to do and they said, "It's yours, run it."

This was a dream come true, the centre consisted of an office, a very large function hall with a large kitchen, a large bar area, a snooker room, a large spare room, a small bar area upstairs and a good size room.

My ultimate vision was to create an area to teach children and adults theatre skills, put shows on in the large function room and have a magician upstairs to teach magic. Students of all ages would come down to the members and practice their table magic. This concept was to increase membership and enhance the centre.

My first task was to re-organise the office. I then told the committee I wanted to build a stage in the large bar area and put on entertainment. This would be on Friday night, Saturday night, and Sunday lunch time and night. The committee said 'refused'. So, I told them if they wanted me to run the centre, they had to trust me and let me do it my way, to which they reluctantly agreed.

I built the stage, booked acts (this took about two months), but it took off unbelievably well. One day the brewery came down to see me, and said they had never seen anywhere with such a big turnaround of bar takings. This initial step that I had taken was tiny compared to what I was aiming for.

One day, out of the blue, I got sacked for no reason whatsoever. The committee thought they could do what I was doing, but they were wrong. The centre, over a short time went back to how it was.

This is why I said, when talking about the village hall (which also applies to community centres), that you should be sure to involve yourself and get onto the committee to safeguard your project, and get members of your group to join the committee with you. This is very important.

Set Design

Page 37 is a plan of a typical hall with a stage, apron, audience seating, and fire exits. To design a set on a small stage such as this, depends what production you are planning. If a one-act play is taking place in one room of a house, this should be quite simple. A one act play with several different scenes however, will require some ingenuity if you are limited to storage space. Obviously, some productions will require specific types of scenery and you could find the area too restrictive. Where possible, I personally like to use black sets and dress them with items to set the various scenes. I like the audience to use their imagination and not be focusing on a small imperfection that may be incorrect.

Page 38 shows a plan of the same venue with the audience facing the fire exit doors. What I like to do is bring the stage into the auditorium as shown. This will restrict audience numbers, so careful calculations are needed regarding finances. Maybe you'll need to put on more performances.

I have put on numerous productions using a raised stage which extended from the main stage to the other end of the hall.

In the 'Pied Piper' play, we used the extended stage and had about 300 rats which travelled from the main stage to the other end of the hall until they fell into the river (which was the bar). The bar still opened in the interval. What we had to take into consideration was the fire exit, which had to remain accessible at all times, so we built over it to keep the access free. The road, which was in front of the audience, had to be designed so that it sloped down towards the audience so the rats could be seen. Page 42 shows sight lines which were crucial to be able to see the rats. If the road was flat, the rats would not have been seen.

Sight Lines

Some set designers don't worry about the audience seeing into the wings, seeing above the stage or the workings at the back of the stage. Some have the curtains open on stage before the audience come in, to let them see the set and get into the atmosphere of the production. Personally, I prefer to go to a show not knowing what's behind the curtains. I don't think there's a better moment than when the house lights begin to fade, the music begins to quieten and as everything goes black and silent, we hear the first sound or the first note of music, and a flicker of light as the curtains begin to open. *Magic.*

I feel the audience should be made to focus on the atmosphere created by lights, sound, and visual content on the stage, whether it be all-black or impressive scenery. Their eyes shouldn't wander to the ropes etc. in the wings, or to the stage lights hanging above the stage (which brings us to sight lines) to keep the audience focused on the production.

We need to draw to scale, the stage and where the audience begins regarding closeness to the stage, furthers from the stage and the two people, left and right in the front row as Pages 41 and 42 show.

If the audience is raked, we need to look closely at the proscenium arch, as this may mask parts of the scenery high up at the back of the stage, which people at the back of the hall may not be able to see.

But let's concentrate on the front row; if they can't see the ropes etc. in the wings, no one else will be able to see them.

Page 41 shows that the audience can't see into the wings. Actors use the wings to enter onto the stage or wait in the wings for their cue to go on. Also, we don't want to see into the green room or those deadly ropes! Page 42 shows a person looking upwards to the ceiling above the stage, where you would normally see the lights or rigging, but this is masked by small flats or curtains. Also on page 42 is the sight line for the 'Pied Piper' rats scene. When a set is designed, you should (using above technique) be able to work out your sight lines and mask accordingly with flats or curtains. Another form of temporary masking, if you can't fly things from the stage, is to use a drop cloth roller system that will mask the stage while changing the set. A roller drop cloth is a long metal tube the width of the stage, which has a canvas sheet rolled around with scenery painted on it; and when released, it unrolls and reveals a painted scene.

Rostra

Rostra to me is essential as it allows you to have different levels and unusual acting areas. If we look back to Page 3, I mention the group I joined at the very beginning of my theatre involvement and said I kept in contact with them and we helped out one another in many different ways. Well, one day, that group got in touch with me and asked if I would like to have all of their equipment due to their centre having to close down. This was amazing, stage lighting, stage lighting control panels, costumes, props, scenery flats, steps, blocks and rostra, which was collapsible. (While I was in the group, I designed and built a hanging system to store the rostra!) To this day some of that group is still together, and they rehearse and put on productions at the centre I created.

I hope you will be as lucky as I was, but if not, look at Page 43 'Folding Rostra'. If you were to make some of these in the sizes I suggest, you will find them really useful and you can bolt them to one another to make them secure. (Bolts are better than screws.) The sides can be filled in with canvas or hardboard or thin ply. (Ply is longer lasting.) Page 44 shows various blocks, steps, etc. Page 45 shows a drawing of a set of steps and a very useful slope. Page 46 shows a detailed manufacturing drawing with cutting list for a four-feet high set of steps. This same method can be used for all items on Page 44. All these items work out so much cheaper to make than hiring in the long run. They will accumulate over time.

Page 47 Scenery Flats

You must use Google for information on how to make scenery flats. There are so many things you can make. From flats with doors in them to flats with windows, you name it! But on Page 47 I've shown the basics, and with experience you will learn what's best. I must mention that on Page 41, if you were to make four flats as high as practical, say 10 feet by 42 inches, and cover both sides with a quarter inch ply wood, these would be so useful if you did a buffet etc. as table tops laid on top of small tables act as support. Regarding scenery flats, you will work out the best way to support them is with hinges, braces and weights etc. Google it!

Stage Models

Once you have your base/venue/centre, what is most useful is to draw to scale your venue in respect to the stage/auditorium etc. as shown on pages 37–40. If possible, draw a scaled model. (Someone in the group would love to do it.) Next, make models to scale of all scenery items on pages 43, 44, 45 and 47. I made all of these to scale using a thick white card (1/16 thick from Hobby Craft), a scalpel and Copydex. All this will help in scenery design.

Set Design
Venue Drawn to Scale ⅛"=12"

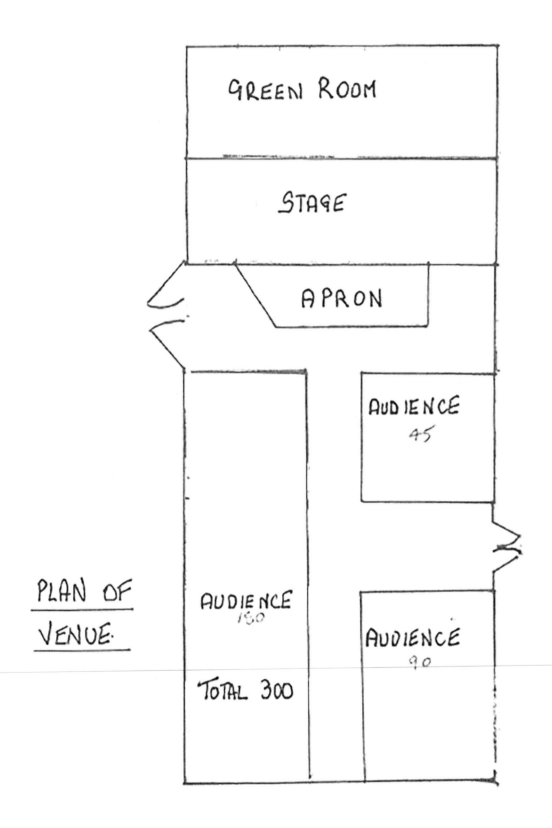

GREEN ROOM

STAGE

APRON

AUDIENCE
45

PLAN OF

VENUE

AUDIENCE
150

AUDIENCE
90

TOTAL 300

Set Design
Empty Space
Scale ⅛"=12"

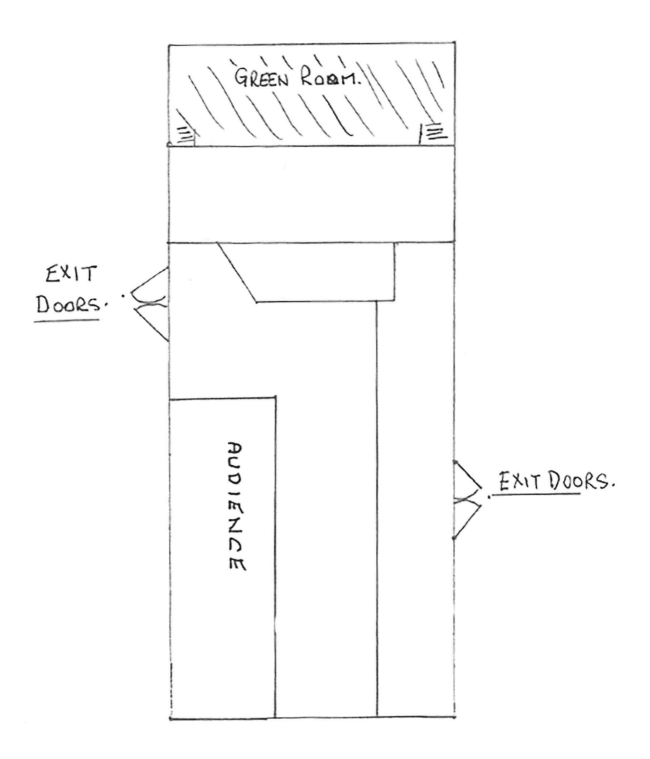

Set Design
Stage Drawn to Scale ¼"=12"

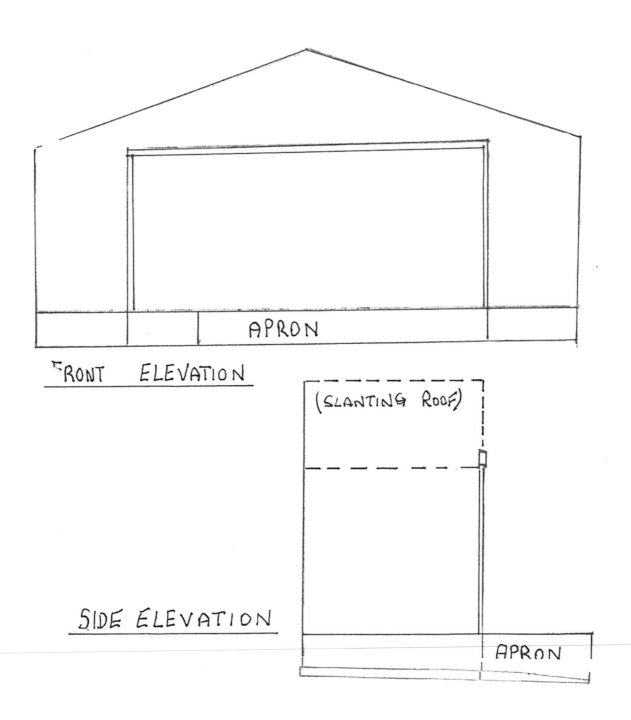

FRONT ELEVATION

APRON

(SLANTING ROOF)

SIDE ELEVATION

APRON

Set Design
Stage Drawn to Scale ¼"=12"

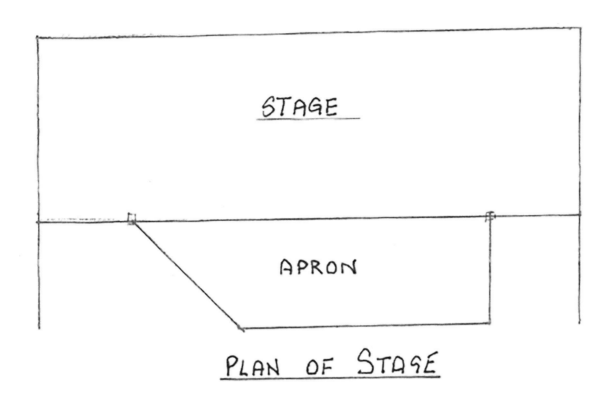

STAGE

APRON

PLAN OF STAGE

Set Design
Sight Lines to Scale ¼"=12"

The chair in this drawing is for height site lines and has nothing to do with this space.

Plan

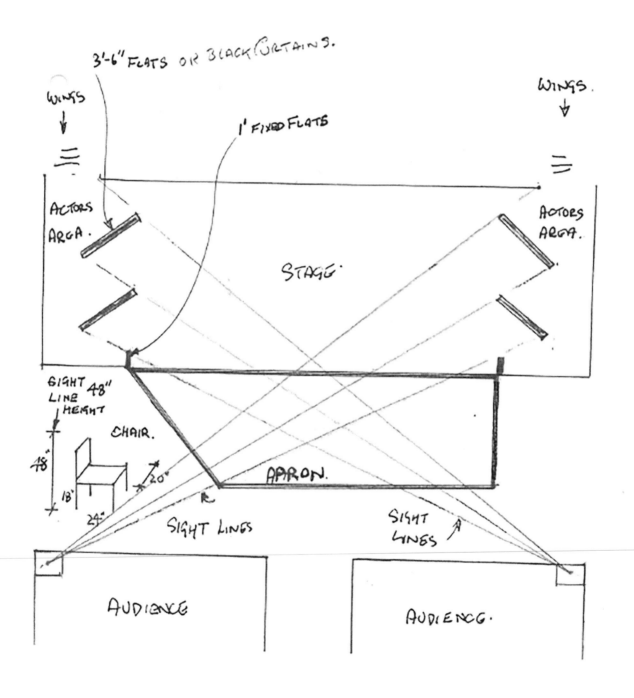

Set Design
Sight Lines to Scale ¼"/12"

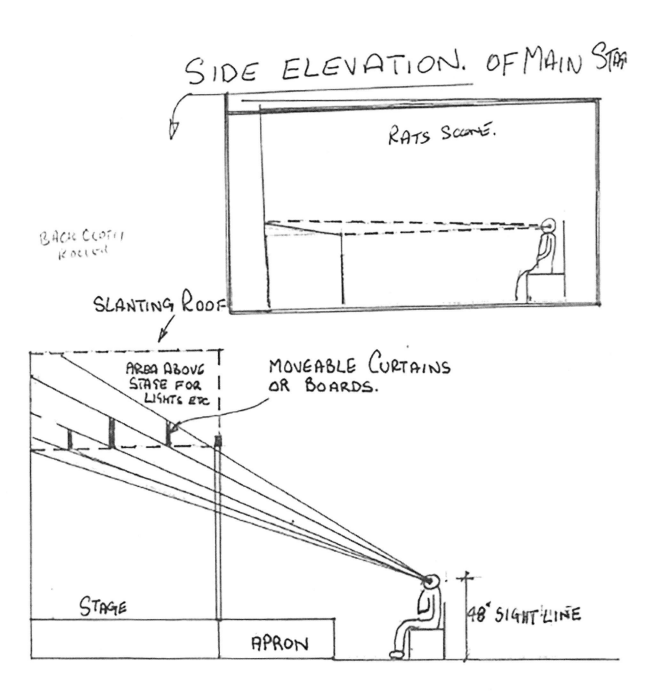

SIDE ELEVATION. OF MAIN STAGE

RATS SCENE.

BACK CLOTH
ROLLER

SLANTING ROOF

AREA ABOVE
STAGE FOR
LIGHTS ETC

MOVEABLE CURTAINS
OR BOARDS.

STAGE

APRON

48" SIGHT LINE

Set Design
Folding Rostra

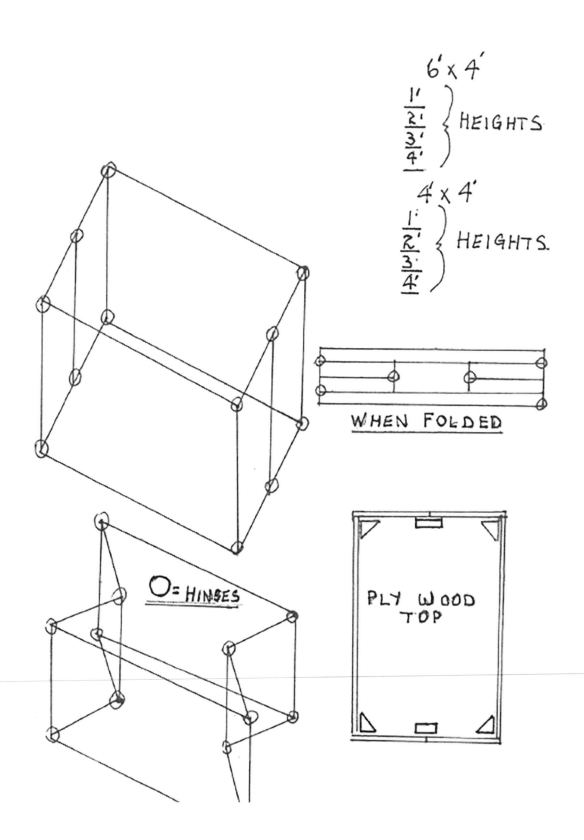

6' x 4'

1' 2' 3' 4' } HEIGHTS

4' x 4'

1' 2' 3' 4' } HEIGHTS.

WHEN FOLDED

O = HINGES

PLY WOOD TOP

Set Design
Useful Solid Blocks and Steps
(No Hinges)

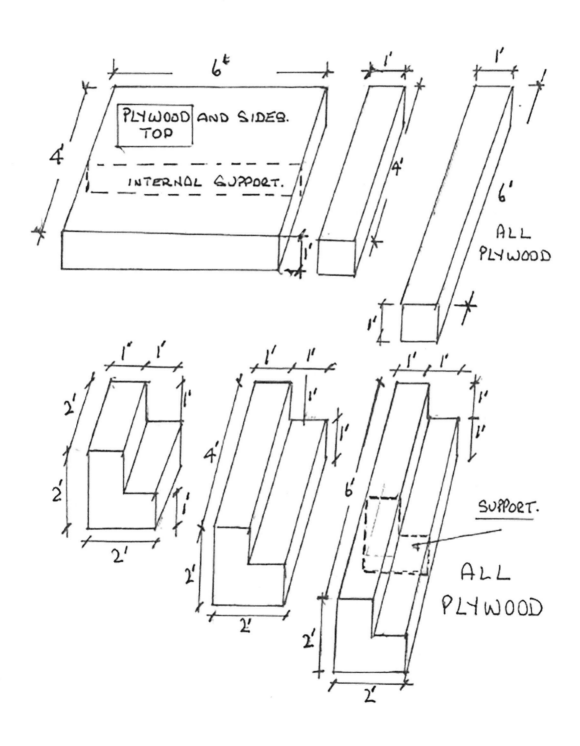

Set Design
Useful Steps and Slope
All Plywood

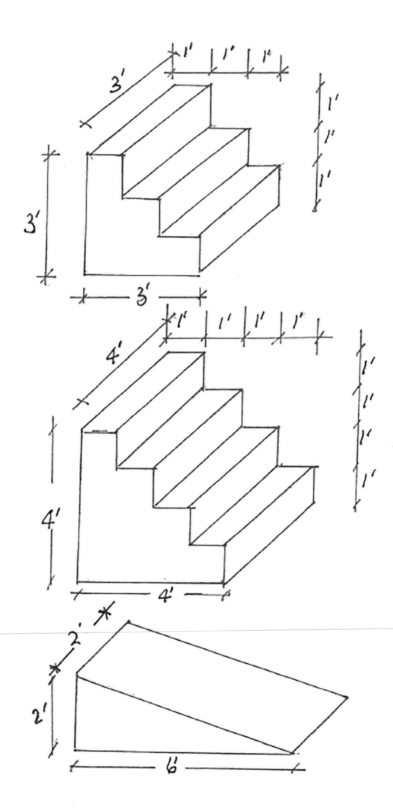

Set Design
Manufacture of Steps

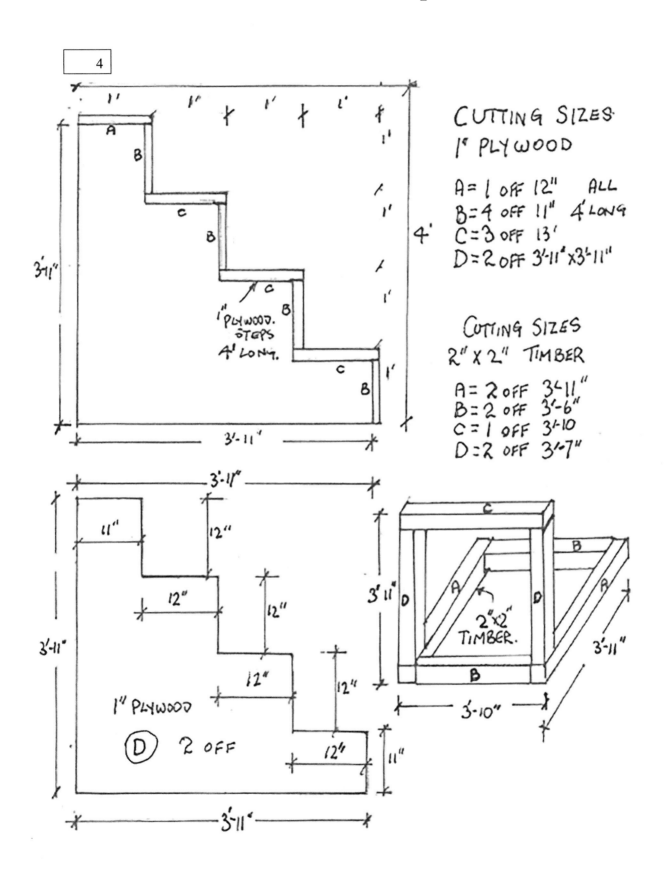

4

CUTTING SIZES
1" PLYWOOD

A = 1 OFF 12"   ALL
B = 4 OFF 11" 4' LONG
C = 3 OFF 13'
D = 2 OFF 3'-11" x 3'-11"

CUTTING SIZES
2" X 2" TIMBER

A = 2 OFF 3'-11"
B = 2 OFF 3'-6"
C = 1 OFF 3'-10
D = 2 OFF 3'-7"

1" PLYWOOD
STEPS
4' LONG.

1" PLYWOOD
D 2 OFF

2"x2"
TIMBER.

Set Design
Flats

Various ways of making flats. If you Google it, it may be easier for you.

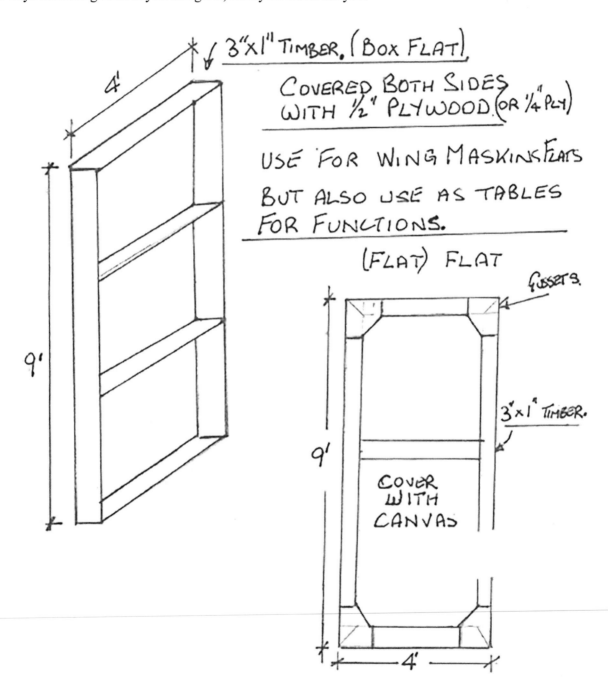

3"x1" TIMBER. (BOX FLAT).
COVERED BOTH SIDES
WITH ½" PLYWOOD (OR ¼" PLY)

USE FOR WING MASKING FLATS
BUT ALSO USE AS TABLES
FOR FUNCTIONS.

(FLAT) FLAT

GUSSETS.

3"x1" TIMBER.

COVER
WITH
CANVAS

4'

9'

9'

4'

Statement

OUR NEXT SECTION IS PROBABLY THE MOST 'IMPORTANT'
YOU ARE AIMING AT PUTTING ON
A
'PANTOMIME'

A play which has every aspect of the theatre within it.

From Slapstick Comedy	Very Sad Songs	Villainous Scenes.
Group Scenes	Love Scenes	Fighting Scenes
Tear-jerking Scenes	Magical Illusions	Special Effects
Audience Participation	Ad-libbing	Improvisation.
Love Songs.		

And Every Possible Characterisation You Can Mention

From 'Shakespeare' To Telling A Joke

If you were a professional production company, with financial backing you would hold auditions for actors, interviews for technical staff, hire equipment, the list goes on!

What you will be doing is introducing absolute beginners that have never been involved in the 'theatre' before to all aspects of the 'theatre'.

So, you need to sort out who is good at what? And who wants to do what?

There will only be a handful of people that will wish to do technical aspects of a production, but many will want to perform. there will be no one left behind, because everyone in the world 'has a gift within them' and you must find it and encourage them to use it.

Introduction to Drama Exercises

The 300 or so exercises that I have listed and from you, allow students access to many situations, and throughout the learning process hopefully develop a team spirit.

The gradual process through the lessons will hopefully create friendships and bonding with one another.

Weekly lessons need to gradually stretch the students' abilities. So, when formulating each session, be aware to add things a little bit harder to do, but also repeat exercises that the students enjoyed or that you feel will benefit them by doing again. They will also feel more confident the second time around.

I am suggesting you do ten-week terms for the school children and a different structure for the adults, one for beginners and one for the experienced members. The experienced members will require less training but help and encouragement from you and good confident direction.

I feel it very important to use music for atmosphere wherever possible in the weekly sessions, especially as they come in to the centre and as they go home afterwards.

I would recommend two warm-up exercises at the beginning of all sessions (except for the adult sessions). They are 'He' and 'Hi what you doing?' At the end of all sessions, you may want to end on a group exercise, but would suggest music as they leave. Make sure it's background music not current music, I've always used classical music as it has a theatrical feel to it.

At the end of each ten-week term, have an open evening and show various exercises. At the end of the evening, I would recommend the whole group perform 'If I were not upon the stage'. It's busy, noisy and visual, and ends the evening with a buzz. (And then put music on as people leave!)

Before we look at the drama exercises, I would like to give some basic tips on mime techniques that may help you during lessons.

In mime, there is an action called 'giving and taking' which is best described in throwing a ball (giving) and catching a ball (taking). As the imaginary ball leaves your hand, you jolt your hand and when you catch the ball, you once again jolt your hand. To understand this jolt, put your left arm up in front of your face and throw the imaginary ball and hit your right wrist onto your left wrist. This is the action you need to show. The same action of putting something onto a table; a little jolt.

When passing objects like a cup of tea, practice with the real object to understand your finger positions; this applies to most mime practices.

Where possible, always keep one hand on an object otherwise the object can disappear.

To open a door, put left hand onto left-hand side of the door frame where the door knob is. With the right hand, turn the knob and open the door, pushing it away from you. Keeping left hand on door frame, lean through doorway keeping door knob in your right hand, and look around the room. Come back out and close the door turning the knob as the last movement.

When drinking a cup of tea or having a drink, look into the mirror and see the lips and facial movements; you will be amazed.

Pulling a rope   The rope is on your right hand side

1. Grab the rope with left hand out front.
2. Grab the rope with right hand about six inches behind the left hand. This is your starting position.
3. Pull rope with both hands until left hand is at your right hip.
4. Keeping left hand on the rope, let go of right hand and reach as far as possible to grab the rope, leaving left hand by your right hip.
5. Let go of rope with left hand, and lean forward as far as possible grabbing the rope with your left hand past your right hand.
6. Pull with both hands and carry on. Practice makes perfect.

Always have at least one hand on the rope at all times.
Believe in what you're doing and look at the rope at all times.

Your next pages describes a coding system. Below is an explanation of how it works. Let's say we use code 1A24.

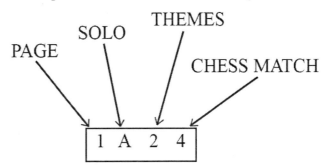

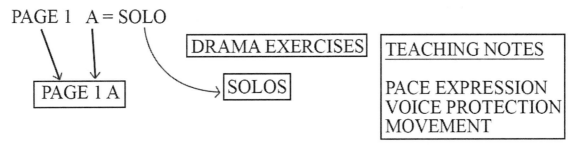

DRAMA EXERCISES
SOLOS

TEACHING NOTES

PACE EXPRESSION
VOICE PROTECTION
MOVEMENT

1 Telephone
Conversations

1 Not Very Interested. Doing Your Nails. Chewing.
2 Won The Pools
3 Sad News
4 Continually Talking
5 Can't Get A Word In Edgeways
6 Your Own Idea

Theme

2 Commentator   1 Very Loud At Football Match   Before The Match

                        2 (As Above)   During Game With Goals.

                        3 Royal Wedding   Very Hushed

Situation   4 Chess Match   Very Hushed

                        5 Boxing Match   During The Fight

                        6 Your Own Idea

3 Compere   1 Introducing:-   Very Loud And Exciting Magic Act.

                        2 Introducing:-   Lady Singer. Quiet Song.

                        3 Your Own Idea

Description Of 'Drama Exercise' Codes

These 'drama exercises' Are the Foundation Stones of The Whole Project. Once The Groups Are Established and You Put on A Full-Length Show, It Will Become So Much Easier and Rewarding to You.

The 'Drama Exercise' Pages Are Not in Any Order Regarding Easy or Hard Situations. You Need to Find What You Think Should Constitute Weekly Sessions. Each Page Of 'Drama Exercises' Has A Page Number and Code Letter on The Left-Hand Side of The Page, And to The Right of This Number in The Middle of The Page Is a Description of The Code Letter. There Are a Total Of five Code Letters Used. Each One Describes the Number of People to Use in The Exercise. For Example:

A = solo
B = two
C = three
D = five
E = whole group

Also down the left-hand side of the page are descriptions of themes. Each theme has a number. To the right of the theme are numbered situations.

So, if we look at page 1a (which is solo) a = solo

Theme 1 = telephone conversations

And number 5 = can't get a word in edgeways

This means that the exercise 'can't get a word in edgeways'

is code 1a15

Question.	What is code	4b14	(look for it)
Answer is	"passing a baby"		

I made this code system to help me keep track of what I used in sessions. You can adapt this to your way or invent your own method. There are over 300 exercises. The next page shows one drama exercise session. It gives the coded exercises to use and the time, in minutes, that they may take.

Study this page and work out the page numbers and where they are.

EXAMPLE OF WEEK 1

52

TIME OF EXERCISE
IN MINUTES

WEEK 1		C	O	D	E	MIN
I	"HE"	9	E	1	1	5
2	"HI , WHAT YOU DOING ? "	12	E	1	1	5
3	BODY RELAX	9	A	1	1	4
4	VOICE PROJECTION. FROM EACH END OF HALL	1	E	2	1	5
5	VOICE FOOTBALL CROWD LOUD THEN QUITE	8	D	1	4	10
6	VOICE LOUD AND SOFT	8	A	1	1	5
7	VOICE BRIDGE COLLAPSE. SHOUT ACROSS RIVER	7	B	1	3	10
8	VOICE HIJACKED WHISPER "WHAT TO DO"	7	B	1	4	10
9	CIRCLE JUMP	12	E	6	1	6

60

WEEK		C	O	D	E	MIN

DRAMA EXERCISES

SOLOS

1 Telephone
Conversations

1 Not Very Interested. Doing Your Nails. Chewing.

2 Won The Pools

3 Sad News

4 Continually Talking

5 Can't Get A Word In Edgeways

6 Your Own Idea

2 Commentator

1 Very Loud At Football Match   Before The Match

2 (As Above)   During Game With Goals.

3 Royal Wedding   Very Hushed

4 Chess Match   Very Hushed

5 Boxing Match   During The Fight

6 Your Own Idea

3 Compere

1 Introducing:-   Very Loud And Exciting Magic Act.

2 Introducing:-   Lady Singer. Quiet Song.

3 Your Own Idea.

IN TWOS

1 Interviews

1 Entertainment Agency

2 Solicitor Requires A Person

3 Boxing Agent

4 Ballet Agent

5 Dynamic American Oil Company

6 Your Own Idea

2 Telephone
Conversations

1 One Loud, The Other Soft (Timid) (Shy)

2 One Listens. The Other Does All The Talking

3 Boss And Employee. Both Loud

4 Burglar Downstairs. Phone The Police

5 Phone For Plane Ticket

Your Own Idea

3 Face To Face
Conversation

1 Two Very La De Da Characters Big Etc

2 Two Very Quiet And Shy Characters

One Loud And One Soft Characters

Your Own Idea

53

PAGE 1 B (Continued)	DRAMA EXERCISES

4 Meeting A Long Lost Friend

1 From Behind And Calling
2 Pass And One Turns Around
3 Pass And Both Turn Around (Timing)
4 On The Phone
5 While Working In An Occupation
6 Your Own Idea

PAGE 1 C	IN THREES

1 Improvisations

1 Park Bench
2 Stuck In A Lift
3 Road Sweepers
4 Council Gardeners

PAGE 1 D	IN FIVES

1 Improvisations

1 At The Doctors. Receptionist. Weird Diseases
2 At The Vets
3 At The Vets. You Are Now The Pet
4 Top Deck Of A Bus
5 On A Plane
6 On A Boat
7 At The Bus Stop
8 Your Own Idea

PAGE 1 E	GROUP

1. If I Were Not Upon The Stage

1 A Bover
2 Sword Fighter
3 Painter
4 Policeman
5 Typist
6 Postman
7 Fireman
8 Pilot
9 Fisherman
10 Chef
11 Referee
12 Wrestler
13 Your Own Idea

2 Voice Projection

1 At Each End Of Hall.   Shout Name
2 At Each End Of Hall.   Whisper

SOLOS

TEACHING NOTES

MIME READING:
BODY MOVEMENT

1 Movement

1 Policeman On Point Duty (Very Rigid. Definite Moves)
See The Vehicles
2 Juggler:– See The Items You Are Juggling (3 Items)
3 Melting Snowman:– Very Slow Gradual Movement Head To Toes
4 String Puppet:– Very Jerky And Swaying Limbs
5 Glove Puppet:– (Use Hand As Puppet) Very Cuddly Movement
6 Knee Puppet:– All Head Moves And Jaw (Mime Putting Puppet Onto Knee)
7 Tight Rope Walker:– Very Precise Steps. See The Rope And Use The Arms.

**2 What Am
I Carrying**

1 Bowl Of Hot Water	(Practice With A Bowl) Fingers
2 Tray Of Drinks	(Practice With A Tray) Fingers
3 Bunch Of Flowers	
4 Baby	
5 Cat	
6 Life Weight Lifters Weights (Barbells)	

IN TWOS

**1 Mirror
Mimes**

1 Make Up
2 Painting
3 Sketching
4 Clay Modelling
5 Decorating The Christmas Tree
6 Operating A Control Panel In An Aircraft
7 Your Own Idea
8 Large Mime. Ballet Exercises

SOLOS

TEACHING NOTES

MIME REGADING:
FACIAL EXPRESSIONS
AND MOVEMENT

1 Magic Box

1 Define The Box And Table

2 Wand

3 Make It Clear What Comes Out Of Box

4 Finish With Closing The Lid. And A Bow

5 Perform An Act

2 Large Magic Box

1 Define The Size

2 Big Wand

3 Make It Clear What Comes Out Of The Box

4 Finish By Going Into The Box And Coming Out As?

3 A Sport Once
Through And
Then Replay
In Slow
Motion

1 Boxing (Knocked Out)

2 Tennis (You Win)

3 Shooting (You Hit Clay Pigeon)

4 Tossing The Caber (It Falls Towards Them)

5 Your Own Idea

4 Walking On:-

1 Hot Floor With No Shoes On

2 Mud (Very)

3 Glue

4 Thin Ice (And Falling In)

Slippery Floor

5 Face And Hands

1 Happy

2 Very Happy

3 Interested

4 Bored

5 Sad

6 Very Sad

7 As If Your Hands And Face Are Freeing From Glue

IN TWOS

With Music

1 Juggler And Assistant

1 Assistant To Enhance The Juggler

Juggler To Convince Us Of The Items

(Above Items To Be Taken From A Box)

2 Snake And
Snake Charmer

1 Snake Lots Of Movement

2 Charmer Very Still   Get Snake From Box

PAGE 4 A

SOLOS

TEACHING NOTES

MIME REGADING:
FACIAL EXPRESSIONS
AND MOVEMENT

1 Mime

1 Chef

2 Model

3 Blind Person

4 Old Person

5 Baby

6 Waiter

7 Deep Sea Diver (Heavy Weighted Boots)

8 Directing A Cranes Heavy Load Onto Lorry

9 Chimney Sweep

10 Your Own Idea

PAGE 4 B

IN TWOS

1 Mime

1 Hanging A Picture

2 Passing A Drink

3 Passing A Cup And Saucer

4 Passing A Baby

5 Passing A Passport To Customs Officer

6 Handing Over A Heavy Bucket Of Cement Not Letting It Touch The Ground

7 Your Own Idea

PAGE 4 C

IN THREES

1 Mime

One Person Speaks And The Others Mime:-

1 Jack And Jill

2   Mother Hubbard

3 Simple Simon

4 Your Own Idea

2 Decorating

1 Painter Plasterer

2 Your Own Idea

Paper Hanger

PAGE 4 D

IN FIVES

1 Machine Using Voices

1 Like A Conveyor Belt, Each Move Motivates The Next, With Sounds

2 An Octopus

3 A Monster (Your Own Idea)

2 A Sport At Ordinary Speed 1 Volleyball

And Then In 2 Netball

Slow Motion As A 3 Football

Replay 4 Cricket

3 A Sport In Mime And Then With Voices. 1 Volleyball

2 Netball

Cutting Voices 3 Football

On And Off 4 Cricket

5 Your Own Idea

PAGE 4 E   GROUP

1   1 Funny Walks Copying The Leader And Then Changing The Leader

2 Demonstrate Outside A Prison And Then Change It To Walking Around An Art Gallery. Freezing Between.

SOLOS

TEACHING NOTES

GAMES RELAXING

1 Begin Miming An
Occupation And
Then Freeze.

1 Ironing
2 Cobbler
3 Black Smith
4 Lumber Jack

Group Guess
The Occupation

5 Conductor Of Orchestra
6 Knife Thrower
7 Your Own Idea

2 Same As Above

1 Karate
2 Wrestling
3 Sword Fighting
4 Javelin Throwing
5 Shot Putting
6 Weight Lifting
7 Your Own Idea

3 Body Actions

1 Show With Foot You Are Angry
2 Trips. (Kicking Your Heel)
3 Fainting

4 Begin A Mime
Then Slowly
Freeze

1 Chopping Wood
2 Digging
3 Bowling At Cricket
4 Bowling Ten Pin

Group Guess
What It Is

5 Tennis
6 Table Tennis
7 Snooker
8 Exercises
9 Your Own Thing

IN FIVES

1 Mime Charades

1 A Stitch In Time Saves Nine
2 Too Many Cooks Spoil The Broth
3 Birds Of A Feather Stick Together
4 It's The Early Bird That Catches The Worm
5 A New Broom Sweeps Clean
6 A Rolling Stone Gathers No Moss
7 Your Own Idea

PAGE 5 E   GROUP

1 Wink Murder   1 Loud Scream

Certain Deaths   2 Singing Sound

                           3 Gun Sound

                           4 Animal Sound

                           5 Quiet Sound

                           6 Your Own Idea

Wink murder, group in a circle, standing.

One person goes into the middle and looks at any person and winks.

The person that is winked at falls to the ground after their noise.

Once all have been murdered start again with new person in middle.

PAGE 6 A   SOLOS   <u>TEACHING NOTES</u>

MOVEMENT WITH
MUSIC FOR FOR
ATMOSPHERE

1 Body Management

1 From Seed To Flower
2 From Hill To Volcano
3 Walking On The Moon
4 An Ant
5 Pulling A Rope On Board Ship
6 Weighing Anchor (Capstan)
7 Moping The Deck
8 Looking Through Telescope
9 Look Out In Crow's Nest
10 Throwing The Lead (To Find The Depth)
11 Fishing With Line
12 Captain
13 Rowing
14 Lion
15 Gorilla
16 Elephant
17 Horse
18 Monkey
19 Tight Rope Walker
20 Clown
21 Lion Tamer
22 Ring Master With Horses

All above should have music or sound effects to give them an atmosphere. Music and sound are very important wherever you can use it.

PAGE 6 D   IN FIVES

1

1 Ants Nest (Discuss Activities)
2 On Boardship (Crew)
3 Machine (Progressive Movement)
With Sound Effects Or Music

2 At A Party Scott

1 Work Out Situation
2 Write It Down

Joplin Music

Practice
Put It On
Tuition

PAGE 6 D
(continued)

3 Orchestra And   1 Decide On Instruments
Conductor   2 Always Watch The Conductor
Mime

Students To Be Seated And When Conductor Points To One Of Them They
Stand And Play The Instrument. Use Strauss Music (Orchestra)

4 Discuss Situations   1 Chimpanzee Tea Party
First   2 Lion Tamer And Lions
                    3 Ring Master And Horses

PAGE 6 E   GROUP

1 Tutor Is Ring   1 Circus Parade. Group Go Round In A Circle And
Master   Tutor Says What You Are
                    And You Become That Animal.

2 Student Is   Circus Parade. Student Says What You Will Be
Ring Master

I Recommend "Entry of the Gladiators" Julius Fucik for the above circus theme items.

PAGE 7 B

IN TWOS

1

1 Is This Your Cat? (Photo) Talk About

2 One Feels Ill. The Other Asks What's Wrong Etc They Don't Know Each Other

3 Bridge Has Collapsed. Shout To One Another Across The River.

4 Highjacked. Whisper. What Do We Do?

5 You Find Treasure. What Shall We Do?

6 Policeman And A Drunk.

7 You Give The Other Person A Big Lottery Win

PAGE 7 D

IN FIVES

1 Improvisation

1 Any Situation Including. Voice. Face. Movement.

The Improvisation Has To Include Shouting, Facial Expressions And Exaggerated Movements.

SOLOS

1 Loud And Soft   1 "Why Hello There, I Must Tell You."

2 Create A Silence (A Pause)   1 "Right"……6 Seconds……"Listen"

3 Create A Mood   1 Happy. "I Feel Really Great Today I Really Do"

2 Sad. "I've No Idea,…… I Suppose One Day We'll Find Out"

3 Frightened. "Don't Move,……Listen….It's In The Wardrobe"

4 Menacing. "You So Much As Blink and I'll Shoot You"

5 Soldier. "Corporal J. Wright, Sir"

6 Vicar. "Today's Service Comes From Somerset"

4 Out Of Space   1 "I Am Kloop, From The Planet Zon"

5 An Animal   1 An Aggressive Gorilla
2 A Gentle Cat

6 Accents   1 Irish "Oh B Jesus, To Be Sure"
2 Scottish. "Hoots Man It's A Bah, Drit, Moon Lit Nit."

IN FIVES

1 Create An Atmosphere   1 A bomb dropping and exploding

2 Wind

3 An angry crowd

4 A football crowd with goals and quiet moments

5 Happy crowd (For he's a jolly good fellow)

6 Your own idea

SOLOS

TEACHING NOTES

FACE AND BODY
RELAXATION

1 Body

Top Half Limp
Gradually Lift Head Up As If On A String
Feel Each Vertebrate Strech

2 Face

1 Purse The Lips
2 Wide Grin
3 Do Both As If Chewing
4 Move Tongue All Over Inside Of Mouth
5 Stick Tongue Out And Touch Chin
6 Stick Tongue Out And Touch Nose
7 Eye Brows Up
8 Eye Brows Downstairs
9 Screw Face Up
10 Strech The Face Skin
11 Hands On Face And Move Skin Over Bone
12 Hands On Scalp And Massage Scalp

Upright

Back Of Head Against Wall Body On Pace Away.
Stay For A Minute
Stay Up And Walk

PAGE 9 E

GROUP

1 He

Give all in group a number. They run around the hall. Call out a number and that person has to touch each person and as they are touched, they have to freeze. Last one to be touched is the winner. If the last person is hard to touch call out three numbers to help.

DRAMA EXERCISES

PAGE 10 A		SOLOS		TEACHING NOTES STAGE TECHNIQUES POSITIONING AND MOVEMENT

1 Techniques

1 Enter Onto Stage, Stop And Face Audience

2 Exit From Stage

3 Head Up. Look Out. Relaxation

4 Stage Trip

5 Fainting

6 Falling

7 Area Names Of Stage

PAGE 10 B		IN TWOS

1 Techniques

1 Stage Trip (One Helps The Other

2 Punch To Others Stomach

3 Receive Punch To Stomach

4 Give A Slap

5 Take A Slap

6 Punch To Other Face

7 Receive Punch To Face

8 Up Staging (Discuss)

PAGE 10 D		GROUP

1 Stage Information

1 Stage Position In A Crowd (Possibly Ad Lib)

2 Stage Position In A Scene (Very Important)

3 Upstaging (Discuss)

4 Stage Entrances

5 Stage Exits

PAGE 11 A

SOLOS

TEACHING NOTES

STAGE TECHNIQUES
OVERLAPING WORDS
AND MOVES.
KEEP IN CHARACTER
AND SITUATION

1 Keep In Your Character
2 Keep Them A Situation
3 Reactions To The Situation

1 Give Them A Character
2 Give Them A Situation
3 Make Something Happen

PAGE 11 B

IN TWOS

1 Overlapping

1 Overlapping Last Two Words When Necessary
2 Overlapping Moves When Necessary

2 Keep Talking

3 Answer A Question With A Question To Keep The Conversation Going.

PAGE 11 D

IN FIVES

1 Reactions

1 Reaction To The Situations
2 Keep In Character
3 Keep In The Situation
4 Be Aware Of What Is Going On.

IN TWOS

TEACHING NOTES

TRUST
MOVEMENT
TEAM
MIME

1 Trust

1 Falling back (into other arms)

2 Sit back-to-back on floor and stand up. Then sit down again keeping back-to-back

2 Movement

1 Standing up make a letter with your entwined bodies.

2 one does a moment and freezes. The other does the opposite.

3 face each other. One makes a face and freezes. The other does the opposite.

PAGE 12 D

IN FIVES

1 Trust

1 Using three groups of five, from 2 line of 7 people facing each other but the stage, (or a platform). Each pair holds hands. The odd person stands on the stage and dives onto their outstretched arms. All have a turn.

2 Observation

1 All in-line shoulders to shoulders, facing front the middle person comes out of line and slowly walks through the gap. The object of this is to show that you can see behind you. They must all stare straight ahead and when the person is out of sight they say, "now" (this is just a bit of fun)

PAGE 12 E (IN CIRCLES)   GROUP

1. "Hi-What You Doing?"   1 Person from circle goes into the middle and keeps doing an action (let's say golf) another person from the circle joins in playing golf (they are now both playing golf) and says "hi-what you doing"? The first person says a different action let's say "kitting and goes back to circle. The person who came out now does 'kitting' and so on all around the circle"

2. Chair   1 Person goes into centre of circle and uses a chair as something (let's say a comb) whoever guesses correct, goes into circle and does something. Tutor decides how long this exercise goes on for.

3. Card   1 Tutor gives a card with an emotion written on it to a student. The student goes into the centre of the circle and mimes the emotion the group have to guess the emotions. The group have to guess the emotion. Groups takes it in turn.

4. TV   1 Person in the middle of the circle is on TV. Group has to guess the programme. All have a turn.

5. Standing Up   1 Group lay on floor in the circle on their backs feet acting centre. All hold hand and stand up. They will have to work out how to do this with their own discussions. (teamwork)

6. Jump And Turn   1 Stand in a circle facing outwards. Tutors called out a sound and after the count of there all jump and face inwards shouting the sound with a gesture.

Types of Shows

Open Evenings. One Hour in Length. (Students' progress)

Each open evening could be regarded as a show; showing and demonstrating things that the students have learnt over the past term and ending the evening with 'If I were not upon the stage'. Why not make it a traditional open evening ending, making sure students use different actions each term.

Money Making Shows.

The more people in a show, the more tickets you will sell. With more children in a show you will sell even more tickets. This approach of making money is very important. Shows are expensive to put on, so you need to build up a healthy bank account. Regarding children, this is not exploitation, you are giving children an opportunity to appear in a show and not charging for pleasure like some large organisations do. They will only be paying their tuition fees. Once you have money in the bank, not only will it help pay running costs, it will enable you to buy extra equipment etc. but most importantly, it will enable you to put on shows that may not make enough money, for example, William Shakespeare, Tennessee Williams, there are many marvellous playwrights, and some students may want to put on one of their plays for the experience.

'Oliver'   'Wizard of Oz'

Both very popular shows with large casts, and they are expensive to put on but capable of making a profit.

Victorian   Music hall

Very popular, enormous amount of material regarding show content. Allows cast to pick many forms of acting. Not too expensive to put on.

Pantomime.

Very traditional, focal point of the year. Can be expensive to put on but should make a profit. If you are able to write your own Pantomime, you could save a lot of money.

'Guys and dolls'.

Well known show, good atmosphere. A challenge to the group.

'Grease'.

Great fun, good music, usually a sellout.

'Bugsy Malone'.

Great opportunity for the young people to have some fun. Great for the family to see.

'Dracula spectacular'.

Great name, popular, and a fun show to be in.

'Jack the ripper'.

Unusual show, great name. Audience puller.

'Match girls'.

Good show, historical facts, interesting set.

'Mayhew's London'.

My own script and all new songs. Eighty in the cast, all historical facts. Ideal for school connections. Stories from Old London at the same time as Charles Dickens.

The other way to use a space is to divide it up and experiment.

As shown in (Drawing G on page 80) I made full use of black curtains (they are a must) and divided our centre into three acting areas.

Stage 1 on our normal stage. Stage 2 and 3 into two smaller stages. We were very restricted to audience numbers but it was an interesting idea.

We performed three one act plays. The audience watched stage 1, then had an interval. They then watched stage 2 and had an interval, then finally watched stage 3.

The audience couldn't see the other sets and had to move from one to another. All three sets were fixed which made it very easy. (No scene changes.)

To us it was very worthwhile. (I repeat this on page 81.)

Above are a few of the many shows available that you could put on. When you search in libraries, book shops, or online you will have such a choice of musicals, full length plays etc. Happy hunting, and see as many live stage productions as possible, both professional and amateur.

Stage Areas
And
Crowd Scene Plotting

When students are first introduced to working on a stage, it can be confusing when the director says, "Enter up stage left and go to down stage right." The reason for this is, direction is given from the audience's perspective, and if you are standing at the same place as the director, it's all back to front.

What I've done is, drawn a plan of the stage the way the actors see it, with a list of basic stage areas. (Drawing A.)

It can get more confusing when the director says, "Move to down house right." This is the audience's view of right, you actually move down stage left!

I personally like to draw a grid onto the stage plan and give each square a number, this also allows more stage positions with more accuracy. Give each actor a copy.

I have drawn a stage with a grid and numbers (Drawing B.) I've included the wings, in case needed to enter or exit from a particular area.

(Drawing C) Shows the stage and apron with the audience sideways because we are going to use half of the hall for our set.

On certain sets it becomes difficult regarding stage terminology, as I have shown (Drawing D).

(Drawing D) is the layout of my production of 'Mayhew's London' a musical a bit like 'Oliver' with a cast of 80 people.

This production consisted of six large crowd scenes so I decided to do a grid system. I've never been involved in a production that uses a system like this before, and I thought *what a good idea.*

I have been involved in many crowd scenes and they usually end up with people standing about, not knowing what to do. Using this technique with a model or a drawing of the stage with a grid like sheet 'D' and using pieces of card with the characters written on them, you can place the actors where you want. Also, this is a check that you have used all the relevant people. So, let's do the exercise.

If you look at (Drawing E) you will see a list of characters that are being told to 'exit' during the last verse of the song *London.* As you sing the words 'When you're feeling down', start exiting as instructed. See if you can work it out.

Using this technique, you can work out entrances, exits, business, and give actors time to study their moves.

Example: Using Drawings D and E, the characters Mick, Ned and Andrew are part of a gang. The director wants them to plot a robbery on stage during a crowd scene. During their entrances, they steal from various people (pick pocketing) until they all meet together at G on the grid and all chat.

Their entrances are: Mick enters from point A, goes up the steps at '15' steals at '11' (from designated person) goes to '6', talks to designated person and then goes to G on his own.

Ned enters C from '11' to '15' steals from designated person, goes down steps, talks to someone (designated) and walks quickly to G to Mick where they chat.

Andrew enters T, steals from designated person at F and goes to G with Mick and Ned. (They all had specific cues to enter, steal and go to 'G'.) They all exit their own way on cues from sheet 'E'. Check it out.

This technique allows a large crowd scene to be acted out without a rehearsal.

It saves time. Gives actors a purpose and all looks natural.

The director is then able to see if his idea has worked and can adjust as required.

GIVE ALL ACTORS A PLAN.

GIVE ALL ACTORS MOVES LIST.

GIVE ALL ACTORS THINGS TO DO.

Sheet 'F' shows photos of the construction and use of rostra, steps etc. using different levels and the audience floor space.

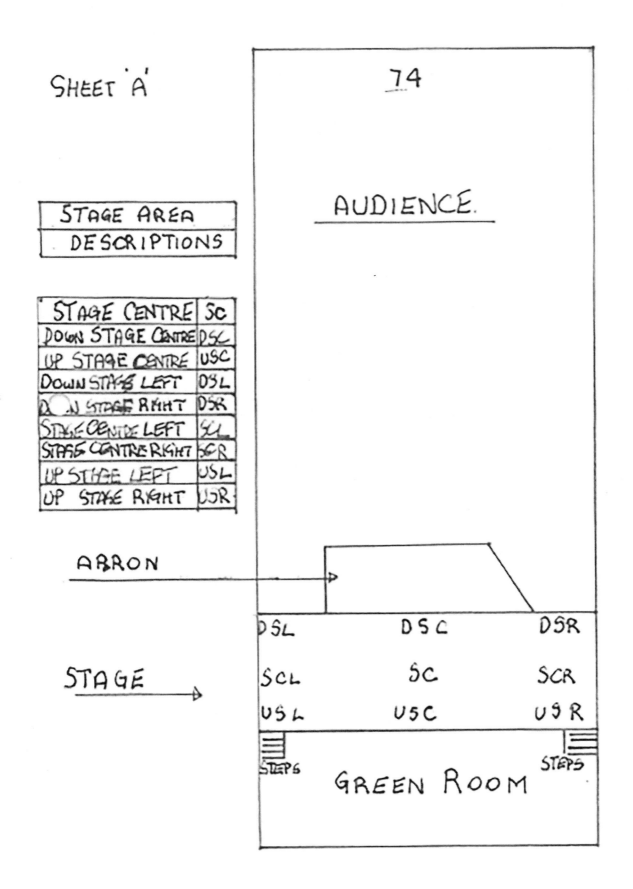

STAGE AREA
DESCRIPTIONS

STAGE CENTRE	SC
DOWN STAGE CENTRE	DSC
UP STAGE CENTRE	USC
DOWN STAGE LEFT	DSL
DOWN STAGE RIGHT	DSR
STAGE CENTRE LEFT	SCL
STAGE CENTRE RIGHT	SCR
UP STAGE LEFT	USL
UP STAGE RIGHT	USR

74

AUDIENCE.

APRON

STAGE

DSL	DSC	DSR
SCL	SC	SCR
USL	USC	USR

STEPS   STEPS

GREEN ROOM

STAGE AREAS

Sheet B

Set Design

Stage drawn to scale
1/4" = 12"

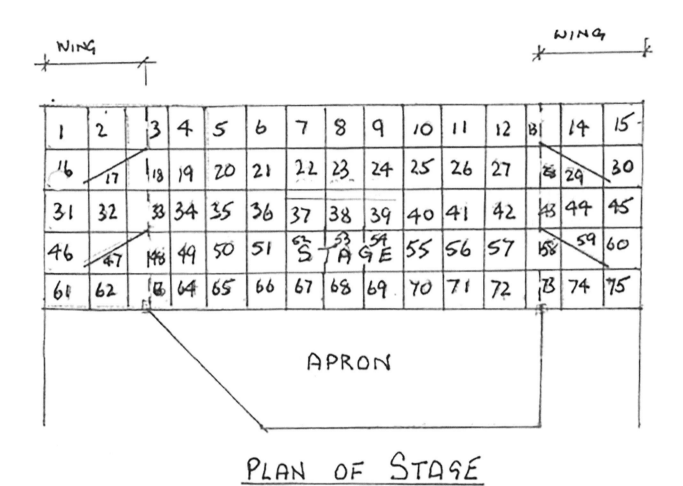

PLAN OF STAGE

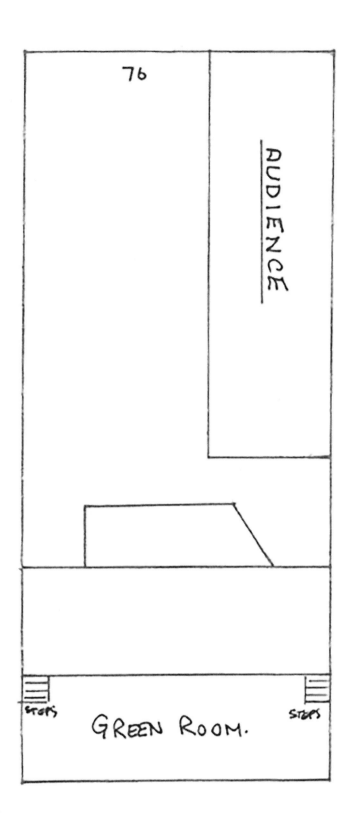

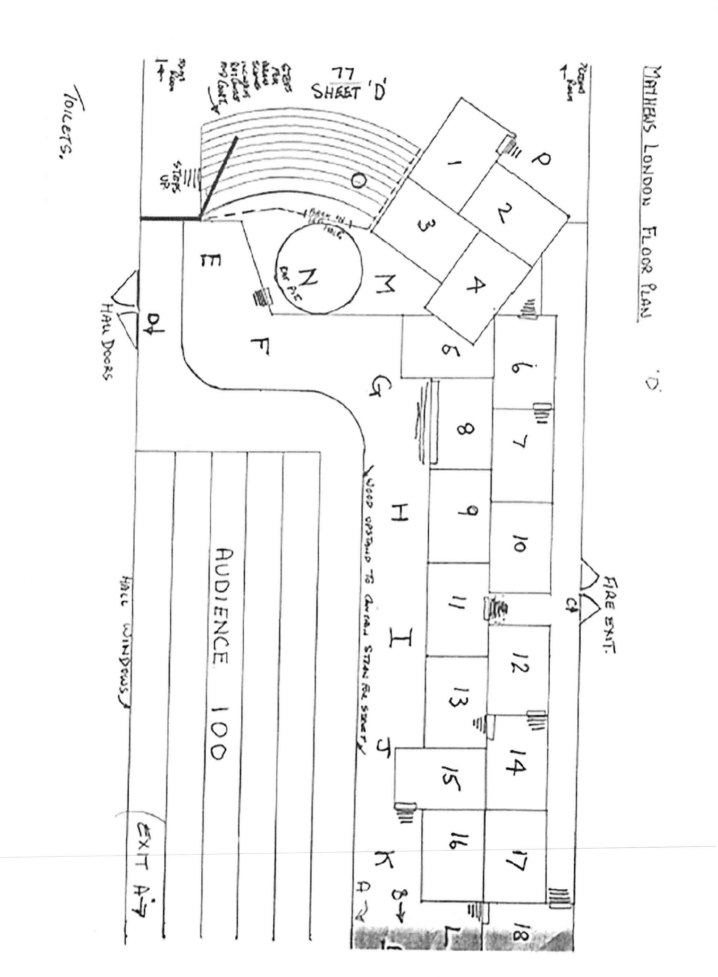

MAYHEWS LONDON MOVES.
78
MOVES FOR "LONDON" SONG PAGE 50

DURING LAST VERSE OF "LONDON" WHEN YOU SING "WHEN YOU'RE FEELING DOWN" MOVE AS BELOW.

CHARACTER	FROM	GO TO	EXIT
BILL	H	A	A
CRESS SELLER	K	F	D
JOE	G	1	1
MICK	K	G	1
INN KEEPER	I	A	A
NED	11	G	D
CHARLIE	E	3	1
ZOE	16	G	D
SWEEPER	10	K	A
DEBBIE	15	5	D
MARY	8	1	1
MAID	J	K	A
GILES	K	A	A
ANDY	5	F	D
EMILY KLAGG	7	15	A
LESLEY	13	K	A
CARA	J	A	A
JACK	7	F	D
KAY	G	D	D
ANDREW	15	G	D
NNY	F	K	A
SARAH	3	1	1
BERT	M	1	1
BET	9	K	A

CHARACTER	PAGE	ENTER	GO TO	EXIT
JUDGE	50	18 (ON 2nd CALLS)	14	18 p51
BOB BOLTON	"	" "	"	" "
MAYHEW	"	" "	"	18 p52
NEWTON	"	" "	"	" p 51
SIMPSON	"	" "	"	" "

USE OF
ROSTRA

USE OF
ROSTRA

MAKING SEATING FOR COURT
SCENE AND RAT CONTEST

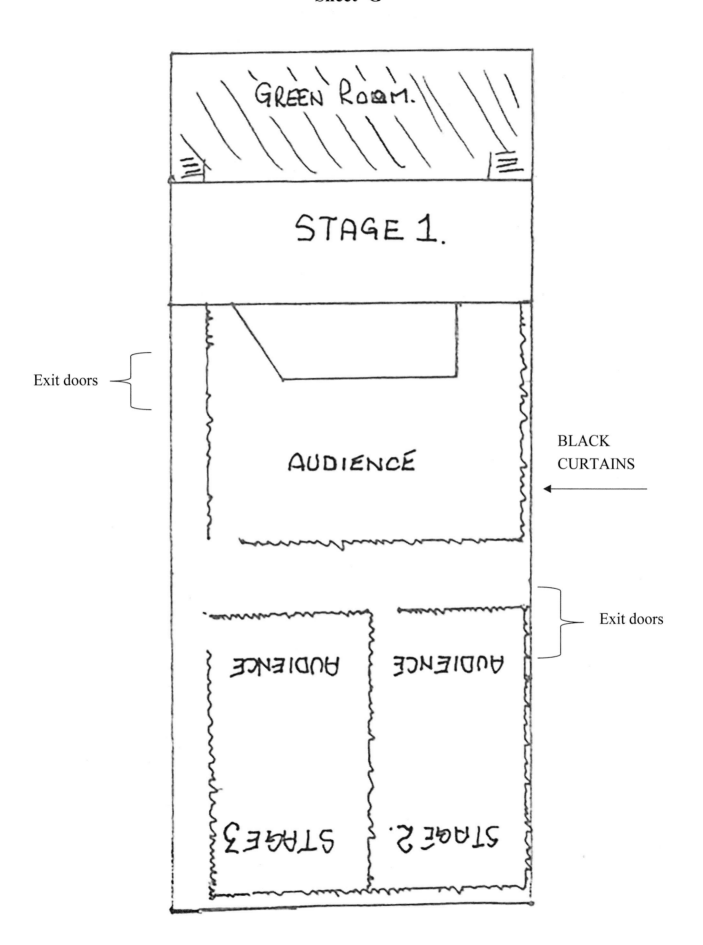

Using Black Curtains

THREE ONE ACT PLAYS

The other way to use a space is to divide it up and experiment.

As shown in Drawing G, I made full use of black curtains (they are a must) and divided our centre into 3 acting areas.

The stage proper. And 2 and 3 into two small acting areas. We were very restricted to audience numbers, but it was an interesting idea.

We performed 3 one act plays. The audience watched stage 1 then had an interval. Then watched stage 2 then an interval. Then finally watched stage 3.

The audience couldn't see the other sets and had to move from one to another.

All three sets were fixed sets which made it very easy (no scene changes).

To us, it was very worthwhile.

Writing Sketches
And
Improvisation Techniques

The useful thing about improvisations is that you can gain ideas that you may use another time. A good idea is to have a pen and paper on hand and write down interesting occurrences for future reference. (This could be in 10 years' time!)

If asked to do an improvisation it can be very difficult to start.

Some people love to be put on the spot and some people hate it.

But the time may come when you're on stage and something goes wrong. This is where improvisation becomes a reality. How do we get out of this situation and keep the scene going?

I remember being on stage with another person acting away as you do, when suddenly the phone rang and it wasn't supposed to. Now, this isn't really a problem, one of you just has to pick up the phone and say 'sorry, you've got the wrong number', but when the phone rang, I looked at my fellow actor for support and all he did was look away, making it obvious I was to deal with this problem. Now, I know I shouldn't have done this, but I thought, you so and so and picked up the phone and said "hello" and then passed the phone to him and said, "it's for you," and enjoyed watching him handle the situation.

It's always a good idea if you can understand the play you are in, so that if a person cuts lines out or goes back in the script you may be able to save the day and improvise.

There have been many very famous sketches created by improvising a situation.

All you need for an improvisation is a group of people sitting in a circle and see what happens, or you could throw an object into the circle and see what happens. This can really bring results, but if you need a bit of help; what I've done in the past with a group of five people is to give one person an occupation, and the other four an item picked out at random. Then give the group, at random, a situation, a first line said by anyone in the group to start the improvisation and the group to portray an emotion regarding the situation.

On the next few pages there are more than enough choices for you to choose from. I will be producing a book, which will contain many thousands of ideas. There are actually 3375 possible combinations within the next few pages. See if you can work them out!

Categories of Improvisation Items

I would suggest you have a look at the next six pages briefly, to help understand what I am about to describe.

Below are categories that you can choose improvisations from. The reason to categorise and number subjects is so that you give new subjects out each time. (You need to keep a record of what you give out.) Try and collect the cards that you give to each person and put them back into their relevant envelopes or boxes.

I personally used thick card to write the subjects onto.

Sheet xi =	Occupations numbers	1−30
Sheet x2= items:	1a=men's clothing	1−15
(3 pages)	2b = women's clothing	1−15
Page 1	3c = cooking utensils	1−15
	4d=cooking ingredients	1−15
	5e=to do with your person	1−15
Page 2	6f= fruit	1−15
	7g=desk equipment	1−15
	8h=transport	1−15
	9i=tools	1−15
Page 3	10j=buildings	1−15
	11k=musical instruments	1−15
	12l=illnesses	1−15
Sheet x3=	Situations	1−30
Sheet x4=	1st lines	1−15
Sheet x5=	Emotions	1−15

When giving a group of five people subjects to improvise with, ask one person to pick a number from 1−30 on sheet x1 (an occupation).

Then, ask the other four people individually to choose from a-l and then a number between 1 and 15 from sheet x2 (an item).

Ask a person a number from 1−30 sheet x3 (a situation).

Ask a person to choose a number from 1−15 sheet x4 (a 1st line), give it to anyone and this starts the improvisation.

Ask a person a number from 1−15 sheet x5 (an emotion) and the group will have to portray this emotion, and when performed, the group watching has to name the emotion.

X1

3 Occupations

1. Dentist

2. Policeman

3. Nurse

4. Doctor

5. Archaeologist

6. Builder

7. Gardener

8. Cook

9. Chef

10. Barber

11. Actor

12. Pilot

13. Car mechanic

14. Carpenter

15. Electrician

16. Plumber

17. Optician

18. Butcher

19. Painter

20. Robber

21. Escaped convict

22. Wrestler

23. Boxer

24. Magistrate

25. Jeweller

26. Cobbler

27. Key cutter

28. Chemist

29. Scaffolder

X2

ITEM LIST

1A	2B
MENS CLOTHING	**WOMENS CLOTHING**

	MENS CLOTHING			WOMENS CLOTHING
1	Suit		1	Suit
2	Trilby		2	Skirt
3	Bowler		3	Blouse
4	Flat cap		4	High heels
5	Wellington boots		5	Tights
6	Shirt		6	Belt
7	Tie		7	Fur coat
8	Belt		8	Stockings
9	Shoes		9	Gloves
10	Socks		10	Hat
11	Scarf		11	Cardigan
12	Overcoat		12	Slippers
13	Waist coat		13	Boots
14	Gloves		14	Jacket
15	Vest		15	Petticoat

3C	4D
COOKING UTENSILS	**COOKING INGREDIENTS**

	COOKING UTENSILS			COOKING INGREDIENTS
1	Knife		1	Salt
2	Fork		2	Pepper
3	Spoon		3	Flour
4	Bread knife		4	Milk
5	Masher		5	Butter
6	Whisk		6	Onion
7	Ladle		7	Garlic
8	Frying pan		8	Wine
9	Saucepan		9	Vinegar
10	Wooden spoon		10	Tomatoes
11	Knife sharpener		11	Honey
12	Sieve		12	Cream
13	Potato peeler		13	Worcestershire sauce
14	Cheese grater		14	Oil
15	Skewer		15	Herbs

X2

5E

THINGS TO DO WITH YOUR PERSON

1	Paint Nails
2	Cut hair
3	File Nails
4	Wash hair
5	After shave
6	Make up
7	Beard
8	Moustache
9	Pipe
10	Pierce ears
11	Razor
12	Tweezers
13	Brush
14	Comb
15	Handkerchief

6F

FRUIT

1	Apple
2	Orange
3	Pear
4	Banana
5	Tangerine
6	Grape
7	Kiwi
8	Grapefruit
9	Lemon
10	Lime
11	Plum
12	Peach
13	Cherry
14	Gooseberry
15	Pineapple

7G

DESK EQUIPMENT

1	Pen
2	Pencil
3	Writing pad
4	Phone
5	iPad
6	Laptop
7	Pencil sharpener
8	Rubber
9	Paper clip
10	Hole pinch
11	Blotter
12	Mouse
13	Stapler
14	In-tray
15	Out tray

8H

TRANSPORT

1	Car
2	Push Bike
3	Motor Bike
4	Bus
5	Coach
6	Cab
7	Plane
8	Ship
9	Roller skates
10	Scooter
11	Skis
12	Snowboard
13	Ice skates
14	Ski lift
15	Horse and cart

X2

9 I
TOOLS

1	Hammer
2	Chisel
3	Screwdriver
4	Pliers
5	Pinchers
6	Hack saw
7	Square
8	Tape measure
9	Roller
10	Drill
11	Chain saw
12	Welding machine
13	Mole grips
14	Sander
15	Sledge hammer

10 J
BUILDINGS

1	House
2	Flat
3	Mansion
4	Temple
5	Church
6	Post office
7	Bank
8	St Paul's
9	GPO Tower
10	Tower of London
11	Palladium
12	Police station
13	Swimming pool
14	Shed
15	Aircraft hanger

11 K
MUSIC INSTRUMENTS

1	Piano
2	Organ
3	Keyboard
4	Trumpet
5	Violin
6	Harp
7	Mouth Organ
8	Guitar
9	Drums
10	Double Bass
11	Clarinet
12	Flute
13	Saxophone
14	Hurdy-gurdy
15	Bag pipes

12 L
ILLNESSES

1	Head Cold
2	Flu
3	Headache
4	Migraine
5	Nose Bleed
6	Small pox
7	Dandruff
8	Eczema
9	Bruise
10	Cut
11	Scratch
12	Sty
13	Sprained ankle
14	Bad back
15	Sore throat

X3

SITUATIONS

1 LIFT

2 CABLE CAR

3 POLICE STATION

4 HOUSE

5 MANSION

6 MUSEUM

7 HOSPITAL

8 CAVE

9 CELLER

10 SEWER

11 LOFT

12 CHIMNEY

13 LIBRARY

14 COURT

15 IGLOO

16 ON TV NEWS

17 INTERVIEW

18 EXAMINATION

19 ON RADIO

20 ON TV QUIZ

21 ON PHONE

22 IN DODGEM CAR

23 AT DOCTORS

24 SUPERMARKET

25 VETS

26 CEMETERY

27 LOST PROPERTY OFFICE

28 CHURCH

29 ON A TIGHTROPE

30 STUCK ON THE LONDON EYE

	X4			**X5**	
	"1ST LINES"			**EMOTIONS**	
1	There's 4 left		1	Happy	
2	It's on there		2	Sad	
3	Put it on this		3	Laughing	
4	You're always arguing		4	Curious	
5	That's brilliant		5	Terrified	
6	You must be joking		6	Puzzled	
7	I've lost it		7	Hot	
8	Tomorrow at 6		8	Cold	
9	Not till we've eaten		9	Bruise	
10	That's the last one		10	Tired	
11	Well		11	Drunk	
12	Say something		12	Winner	
13	We've done it twice		13	Loser	
14	Only you		14	Breathless	
15	Ask him		15	Got to be quite	

Stage Makeup

Stage makeup can be expensive, so ideally the students should buy their own box of makeup; they will eventually need it. If organised, a basic collection of makeup could be bought and shared by the group until people obtain their own.

What a great birthday or Christmas present!

Why use makeup	Without makeup the stage lights will pick up perspiration. This will make the face shine and mask facial features.
	With makeup you can highlight features on the face such as eyebrows, cheek bones, lines, lips etc. and afterwards when you powder down, this will eliminate the shine on the face.
An ageing person	If wanting to age a person, it's important to use makeup on the hands. Enhancing veins and powdering down.
Spotlight	Use a spotlight to show the difference from perspiration to powdering down after applying makeup.
Buying stage makeup	Leichner is a popular make of stage makeup.
Makeup books	There are many stage makeup books. I found stage makeup by 'Herman Buchman' very useful.
Wax and Putty	To enlarge noses, or make moles, lumps, scars, cuts etc. Example of a two-inch cut:
	Roll a piece of putty the shape of a pencil two inches long, and press it onto the skin where you want the cut to be. Squash the edges of the putty into the skin to get rid of the joint to the skin. With a toothpick or matchstick, cut a groove into the putty to create the cut. With makeup, colour the cut and surrounding area, putting red makeup into the cut and lightly around the surrounding area to create bruising effect. Powder down.
	Put some red makeup into the cut and add some removing cream to give the effect of wetness. Then use stage blood for the final effect.

Cut off Finger	Bend index finger to make it look like it's been chopped off. Put some putty onto the end of the bent finger and smooth it onto the finger and make the end look like the bone. Make it up as you did the cut above.
Facial Hair	To create beards, moustaches etc. use crepe hair from the company 'wrath wool crepe hair' and hair glue. When you buy hair, it will be very curly. To straighten it out, boil a kettle, and when it steams hold the hair over the steam and it will straighten.
Gaps in teeth	To look as though you have lost some teeth, use black tooth enamel for the stage.
Loss Or dropped Eye	Glue gauze over eye socket (not touching eye lid be careful) and use makeup over it to have no eye, or use a ping pong ball fixed to a string as a hanging out eye, or glue half of the ball onto the cheek bone like Quasimodo (the hunchback of Notre dame)
Plaster of Paris regarding moulds for the face	This technique requires you to get correct information before attempting this procedure.

I'll give the basic principle regarding face moulds but do not attempt it until you get correct information.

Ideally, you should have a full-face mould of your face, and then any characteristics you want to add will be easy to make and this mould will last forever.

Put some Vaseline all over your face. Put a pad of cloth over eye sockets for protection. Put a good layer of plaster of Paris over face, put straws up nose to enable you to breathe. Leave on the face until it dries. You will need someone to do this for you.

When plaster of Paris is removed, clean inside of the mould and remove loose particles.

Put plenty of Vaseline inside of mould covering all of inside and then completely fill the mould to the top, making a solid mould of your face. Leave overnight and when completely dry, break the mould apart and you will have a cast of your face.

Make a funny nose	Put putty onto the cast and make the shape you want, making sure you smooth the putty to prevent a joint seam. Paint the putty with latex or try Copydex. When dry, peel off and glue to your face.
	Now you are able to make a full mask of your face however you want it to look. Have fun.
Blood Capsules	Blood capsules are used to create a bleeding mouth or a vampire blood around the mouth. Capsules are put into the mouth and chewed.
Bottled Blood used	Stage blood comes in small bottles and is there and when required

There are loads of other effects, use Google.

Rehearsal Techniques

I Have Produced Two Detailed Information Sheets
One For a Script Grid
And One for A Rehearsal List

Each character is to have a full rehearsal list. This can be adjusted if required as you progress.

Note: These information sheets are only a small part of a play but hopefully give you the general idea. If you study the rehearsal list against the script grid, you will see how it works. This technique will take a little while to master, but it will be very useful to you including other aspects such as sound and lighting etc.

If you make up small cards (one inch by half an inch) and write the characters' names on the cards and place them next to their names on the script grid (as shown on the information sheet), you will see at a glance who requires a rehearsal slot.

The rehearsal grid needs to be a sturdy board as it will have plenty of use.

These character cards will be used on your set plan or model as you place them during working out your moves.

CAST ↓

94

			SCENE 1 LONDON STREET					SCENE 2 KLASS'S				SCENE 3 SARAH'S LODGINGS			SCENE 4 THE STREET							SCENE 5 SWEEPS LODGINGS	
						MUSIC			MUSIC						MUSIC		MUSIC						
			SONG								SONG		SONG					SONG	SONG	SONG			
	CAST NAMES	CHARACTERS	1	2	3	4	5	6	7	8	9	10	11	12	13	14	15	16	17	18	19	20	21
GILES	JOHN K.	GILES	X	X										X	X						X	X	X
JOE	BEN	JOE	X	X	X	X	X	X													X	X	X
CHARLIE	DANIELLE	CHARLIE	X	X														X			X	X	X
	JILL	SARAH		X	X	X						X	X	X	X	X							X
	JANE	JACK		X	X	X	X	X											X				X
	LESLEY	LADY 1				X					X												
	CARA	LADY 2				X					X												
	LISA	MAID						X	X	X							X						
	ADAM	BERT						X	X	X										X			
	HADLEY	NED							X	X						X					X	X	X
	PETER	GAFFY							X	X						X					X	X	X
	DON. H.	MR. KLASS							X	X									X				

REHEARSAL LIST
95
IF YOU CAN'T MAKE A REHEARSAL PLEASE PHONE

DAYS AND DATES	ACTING		SINGING.		
JAN 4TH MONDAY	P1 - 6	7·30 - 9·00	BERT P13	7·30 - 8·00	
	P6 - 8	9·00 - 10·30	LADIES P9	8·00 - 8·30	
			SARAH P11	8·30 - 9·00	
			GILES P1	9·00 - 9·30	
			CHARLIE P16	9·30 - 10·00	
JAN 11TH MONDAY	P10 - 13	7·30 - 9·00	BERT P13 7·30 - 8·00		
	P·13 = 17	9·00 - 10·30			
JAN 18F MON					
JAN 25TH MON					
FEB 1ST MON					
FEB 8TH MON					
FEB 15TH MON					
FEB 22ND MON					
FEB 29TH MON					

My Technique Regarding Keeping the Cast Interested and Enthusiastic Throughout the Rehearsal Process.

Once you have rehearsed all of the scenes in the play, you will know what requires extra rehearsals.

You must keep the cast interested, and I find the best way to do this is keep them in the dark. Thus, never go through the play over and over again from the beginning, it will become tedious and lose its sparkle.

Rehearse scenes completely out of sequence and don't show the links between scenes for as long as possible.

As rehearsals progress and get nearer to the show date, we start putting the play into order of scenes.

The first step is to have a technical rehearsal which goes from the end of one scene and into the next scene. This may take two rehearsal nights as you may have to do the link twice if not correct. This technical rehearsal will create an interest for the cast.

These two technical rehearsals are probably the most important dates of the whole rehearsal process. See if I can explain this.

For us to know the date we have to do these two technical rehearsals, we have to work backwards from our opening night.

See next page.

March	Monday 31st	1st half scene Links	
April	Monday 6th	2nd half scene links	
	Monday 13th	1st half	
	Monday 20th	2nd half	
	Monday 26th	All day	Sort out problem day
	Monday 27th	Once through	Whole show
May	Sunday 3rd	All day to sort out the once through	
	Monday 4th	Full dress	Once through
	Sunday 10th	10 pm once through tec…3–6 full dress	
	Monday 11th	Opening night	

We now know the date of our two-scene link date.

Monday, March 31.

We had our first reading of the play on Sunday, January 3.

Basically, we have 18 weeks of rehearsals.

We have based these rehearsals on using the main hall for acting and a separate room for singing. If we were able to use another space, we may be able to reduce the 18 weeks.

I recommend, before the first reading:

Plan all moves per character and produce copies for actors.

Plan rehearsal sheets ready to give to actors once show is cast.

Plan, if possible, set building times.

Try and find an MD (Musical Director)   See next page

I decided I would like to put on 'Guys and Dolls', and because the music is so well known and we were not an operatic society, I wasn't sure the group were able to put it across.

One evening in the pub, I was talking to some of the group and mentioned the songs and thought the only way we could put it on was to find an MD, "Paul's an md, he's just left university studying music." "Who's Paul?" I said. "The barman." Now Paul was in his early twenties and really didn't look old enough to be an MD. I went to the bar and introduced myself, and asked if he would be interested in getting involved. He jumped at the opportunity.

He came to rehearsals and was amazing. The group had always sang in the shows and could put a song across, but suddenly with his direction and skill, we were singing in harmony and sounded bloody marvellous.

When we went to a friend's studio to record the music, he was asking the sound technician (who was a friend of mine) to alter certain things; he knew exactly what he wanted.

When we put on the show, we recorded the songs. A few weeks later, we bought a cassette of *Guys and Dolls*. We put both tapes in a double cassette player and synchronised them; the cassette we bought was of the national theatre production. It was unbelievable, we turned one down and listened to the other and vice versa, and you couldn't tell the difference. The sounds and the timing was spot on.

I mentioned this story just to show how important an md is, and how they can enhance a show.

You really do have to ask around for people to help your productions; not only will it give you satisfaction but they will also love to get involved.

Cues

Cue sheets for

Sound/music

Lights

Curtains

Scenery

Piano

Special effects

Props (this includes everything from a cup to a sofa)

We will start at the very beginning. (A very good place to start!)

Doors open at	7:30		
Show starts at	8:00		

You put the interval music on at	7:25	sound cue A	(SCA).
You turn out the house lights.			
And bring up softer lights at	7:25	light cue A	(LCA).

This sets the lights and sound

At 8:00	You start the show on "go"	By whoever is in charge.
Sound cue B	(SCB) on 'Go'	Fade out house music.
Light cue B	(LCB) on 'Go'	Fade out house lights.

Both slowly together.

In this instance we will assume that sound will begin the show.

Sound Description

CHE	PAGE	
1	1	As house lights fade out, up music cue 1, 'A dream for us'

Light description

CHE	PAGE		
1	1	Up sweeps 'AND'	Build during the scene.

I've always found, for some reason, that the start of the evening is always the hardest. From now on it gets easier.

Although I'm a member of equity and have appeared professionally on stage, I have never been involved professionally with the technical aspect of professional theatre.

The way I produce cues is the way I have always done. Hopefully, members of the group one day go to drama school and learn the professional method. At least they will have learnt the basics.

Let's get on with it!

All the technical people that I listed at the beginning of this item will have scripts. They will all write their cues onto their scripts, at a technical meeting, where you will give cues from your master script.

(They will understand their own writing.)

You write their cue sheets out beforehand and you all go through the script together.

Procedure for writing cues and descriptions

| We've done cue A | And B | For lights |
| We've done cue A | And B | For sound |

Now let's go through the script only looking at sound and lights.

I've photo copied the 1st page of 'Mayhew's London' and a copy of the sound and light cue sheets.

Carefully go through the script. Read everything, and when you see the reason for a cue write it in. For instance, the scene starts with a song 'A dream for us'. Put sound cue 1 where it says 'A dream for us' and on your sheet write:

As house lights fade out. Up music cue 1 'A dream for us'.

If you decide to bring the lights up as I did underline 'and' then put LC1 bring lights up on 'and'.

Go through the whole script like this.

What you could do, for instance, is use your 'special effects' cue sheet and write page 1 cue 1 at 7-50, go around the stage with a smoke pellet to give atmosphere and write this on script page 1.

Having these cue sheets allows you to go to certain places in the script easily.

SCA LCA
SCBLCB
SC1

Page 1
Act One

Scene One. The Misty Streets of London.

Small sweeps are seen appearing from the mist, tiny frail and hungry.
Music will play during their entrance to set the scene and then into "A dream of us"

OPENING SONG "A DREAM OF US" (the Sweeps)
LC1

In the dark old streets of London
Walking alongside friends
Feeling lonely tried bewildered
And wondering when this will end
Will end, will end, will end

Onward forever onward
Waiting for dark to come
Climbing the filthy chimneys
The last time for some

Etc, etc, etc

Once these initial cues are carried out it gets easier

(chuckle, chuckle, chuckle)

CUE	PAGE	DESCRIPTION.
A	1	Interval Music on at 7-30.
B.	1	Fade Music on "Go"
1.	1	As House Lights Fade out. Up Music Cue 1. A drummer us
2.	6	On "Come on" up Music Cue 2.
3.	9.	On "Oh Yes" up Music Cue 3.
4	11.	On "Later" up Music Cue 4.
5	12	Let Tape Run and into Music Cue 5.
6	16	On "What" up Music Cue 6.
7	17	Let Tape Run and into Music Cue 7.
8	19	On "Wahoo" up Music Cue 8.
9	25	On "Us" up Music Cue 9. (Loud)
10	25	Let Tape Run and into Music Cue 10.
11	26	On "Yeah" up Music Cue 11.
12	27	On "Bingo" up Music Cue 12
13	30	As Lights Fade out on "First" up Music Cue 13.
14	32	On The Camera Finish up Music Cue 14.
15	34	On "Trouble" up Music Cue 15.
16	34	As Lights Fade After Fight (Count 3 seconds and up Music Cue 16.
16A	25	As Lights Fade After Song Count 6 seconds and up Strauss
		Interval.
16B	36	On "Go" Fade Strauss.
17	36	6 seconds After Lights come up in Music Cue 17.
18	38	On "Go!" up Music Cue 18.
19	39	On "Fire" up Music Cue 19.
20	40	On "Sir" up Music Cue 20.
21	42	On "Shut em up" up Music Cue 21.
22	43	On "Few Bob" up Music Cue 22.
23	45	Let Tape Run and into Music Cue 23.

LIGHTS.

CUE	PAGE	DESCRIPTION.
A	1	HOUSE LIGHTS ON AT 7·30.
B	1	FADE LIGHTS ON "GO"
1	1	UP SWEEPS ON "AND" 3rd Dienst Scene.
2	3	FADE SWEEPS AND UP AREA 10 ON "LOOK" AS THEY SEE
3	4	UP SWEEPS ON "JOE".
4	6	OUT SWEEPS AREAS 0 1234 ETC Leave 10 UP ON "LATE"
5	6	AS YOU HEAR "MUSIC CUE 2" FADE LIGHTS. AT END OF MUSIC UP SINGER
6	7	ON "NAUGHTY" OUT 8&9 AND UP KLASS. 14-17 AREAS
7	9	AT END OF SONG (MUSIC CUE 3.) OUT KLASS & UP SARAH AT 6
8	11	AT END OF SONG (MUSIC CUE 4) OUT SARAH & UP ALL STREET.
9	16	AS SWEEPER MOVES TO AREA 11 OUT STREET AREAS. (STARS ETC)
10	17	AT END OF "MUSIC CUE 6" ON "JOE" UP 14-17 & OUT 11 ETC.
11	19	ON "WAHOO" OUT BILL & UP CHIMNEYS 1-4 N-N ETC
12	24	AS THEY GO TO CHIMNEY UP AREA 5.
13	25	"US" FADE CHIMNEYS AND UP 13-18 AREAS way butterflies THEY FINISH AT AREA 5.
14	27	ON "ONLY" ALL OUT AND UP 7 8 9 10.
15	30	ON "FIRST" ALL OUT & UP THE INN WHEN YOU HEAR MUSIC.
16	34	AS ALL FREEZE AFTER FIGHT SLOWLY FADE ALL OUT UNTIL YOU HEAR MUSIC THEN UP FOR FINALYDE.
17	55	AS SONG ENDS ALL OUT Slowly WHEN YOU HEAR STRING UP HOUSE INTERVAL.
18	36	ON "GO" FADE OUT HOUSE LIGHTS UP LIGHTS ON NOISE. INN AREA
19	37	ON "PIT" UP STARS ETC.
20	39	ON "FIRE" FADE OUT THEN UP L-8 AT END OF MUSIC 19
21	42	AS SONG SELLER EXITS AFTER MUSIC CUE 20 ALL OUT AND UP THE INN AREA.

Publicity

People need to know you are there.

People need to know what you are doing.

People need to know about your shows.

Where to advertise

1 Libraries

2 Local Boards

3 Shop windows

4 Papers (Expensive)

5 Article in newspaper.

Get in touch with local papers and let them know you are running a new theatre project for children and adults of all ages on an amateur basis, so fees for all classes will be at minimal cost. Ask if the paper would be interested in an article to let the local community know of this new exciting project.

6 The Internet

7 Youth clubs

8 Churches

9 Drama groups.

Visit local drama groups and make yourself known, and keep in touch with them.

10 An Association

Think about organising amateur group meetings to discuss various ideas or to suggest putting things to the local arts council or the main council. Groups could help each other with equipment and publicity and date of each other's shows so they don't clash. This could be a very productive idea and a feather in your cap.

11 Community Associations

12 Senior Citizen Groups

13 Local Arts Council

Make contact about publicity but the Arts Council will be covered in the next section.

All above items are about local networking.

It's important you study pages 26–29 regarding publicity brochures.

The publicity section we are looking at, at the moment, is for when the project is about to commence taking in students. The brochure for this has to have all the relevant classes' aims, contact details etc. but will have no logos from the arts council or the main council. Brochures that will have logos (we hope) will be mainly for schools.

Recap 1	Pages 9-25	POSSIBLE BROCHURE DESIGNS
2	Page 28	A very basic brochure to show to arts council and schools to get their reactions.
		Regarding schools, this is not to try and get into schools; we are only looking at their reaction to what we are doing. Try and talk to a school that is interested in the theatre. A very brief chat. Ask if there are any youth centres in the area.
3	Pages 26–29	Produce a proper brochure to hand out to everyone (except schools).
4		Once you are established, try and get your logos which will allow you into schools. Ever so important. You will have to produce more brochures, so in your original design, allocate a space for them. This shouldn't cost much more.

Also, this brochure for schools has to have on it:

'We offer as an introduction, a full or half-day workshop at your school.'

Also mention to the head teacher that you are able to put on a show for the PTA at a very reasonable price. Maybe a 'Victorian music hall'.

Publicity
(Continued)

Once you are established and recognised as a reputable organisation

Once you are established, you will have a track record and be known by many people, and hopefully have built up a good reputation. If you haven't, best pack up and get a job!

Okay you've done an excellent job. Now we can, with confidence, take the next step and approach far more people.

See if the local paper has an arts critic. If they have, ask if they would like to come to your shows and comment. If no critic, ask if they would produce a write-up for the paper.

You can invite the mayor to a show. (And the paper.)

You can invite charitable organisations (and the paper)

Youth centres.

Either yourself, or a person that takes on publicity needs to get involved with the local arts council secretary or main council arts department. Let's assume there is an arts council secretary.

By now you will probably know the secretary, ask him if it would be possible to have an arts council logo for your brochures as you are providing a good facility for the local area, and that you would like to approach local schools regarding introducing young people to many theatre skills. Also, ask where you can advertise your brochures locally.

Ask for a list of amateur drama groups including dance schools.

Go to all arts council meetings and volunteer.

Make contact with the arts council chairperson.

Go to all arts council meetings and volunteer.

Main council arts department make contact ask about their logo same idea as arts council discussion.

Schools

We are focusing on young people in schools; we believe this project will give them a chance to get involved in an activity that has so much involvement and also has an end product; a show. During this process, they will learn many skills, too many to mention here, but will be taught as they proceed through the project.

Schools are our main source of members and obviously our main source of income, but more importantly our main source of publicity. If you can create a relationship with local schools, you will be reaching out to thousands of people that will have an opportunity to get involved in a new project, whether it's seeing a show, a theme evening, helping with the project or just watching their children develop in so many ways.

A brochure taken home by one school child will reach mum, dad, brother, sister, grandad, grandmother, uncle, aunt. This is just 8 people. Each of these people have contact with at least one other person which now equals 16 people. Let's say an average class has 20 children, this means, every 20 children could reach 320 people. If we say an average school has 140 children (this is a very small number!) this will equal 140 divided by 20 = 7 classes 7 × 320 = 2240 or 140 pupils × 16 contacts = 2240 potential receivers of your publicity per school. This will not only advertise your classes but all your shows and special events. You must be well organised and have very good quality tuition and shows etc., as near to professional standards as possible.

Mention special events to catch the eye of teachers and head teachers, for example:

Basic brochure 1st page

Hire a double decker bus or coach and have a backstage visit to the Sadler's Wells Theatre, one of the most famous theatres in London. Learn about the ghost of Sadler's.

Basic brochure back page

Drama workshops for schools. At your school or at our centre. Transport can be arranged.

Brochure hinge 1st and 2nd pages.

Two dancers to visit the centre from the royal opera house. Plus a musician and a set designer from Covent Garden. A workshop for dance and set design.

Brochure staples 4th page.

Drama festival. We enter our play into the local drama festival.

Brochure staples 4th page.

Back stage visit to the national theatre by coach to one of the world's most modern and technically advanced theatres in the world.

Costumes

Most groups end up with someone helping to make costumes for the shows. You will be surprised what people can do.

Our pianist Peter, who played by ear, was out of this world as a pianist, one in a million. One day, I decided to put on a medieval banquet; we already had people that could make costumes but we needed a costume for Gary, our sound expert, the exact shape as Henry the 8th.

This was a complicated costume, and who made it? Peter. It was incredible and after this, he helped out when required (many times) so you will have to be patient.

As you put sketches on, the cast will try and dress for their parts and gradually things will appear, and you will ask, *who made that?* that's where it starts from.

Charity shops, jumble sales or even a small card in a shop window may bring in clothes or helpers, and of course there is the internet.

We could talk about hiring, sometimes you have to hire, but be aware of the cost.

You may find a drama group that will hire out their costumes which would be handy. One day, you may help them out somehow.

If you buy the materials and make your own, it will be so much cheaper in the long run. Also, you have the internet to ask for helpers.

Things will happen. Also, if someone can make costumes for the group, try and get students to help and learn.

Props

Much the same as costumes, you will need people with experience on how to make things, they will appear. Get students involved as it can be very interesting.

Props are anything from a cup to a four-poster bed. In my production of 'Mayhew's London' we needed not one, but two hurdy-gurdies, a hand-held musical instrument with keys and a handle to turn. The reason two were required was because in the play, Sarah, the hurdy-gurdy player (you'll find her in the history books) gets knocked over and she breaks her hurdy-gurdy. Later in the play, she repairs it so we had to have one that played, and one that would break (intentionally).

A friend of Irene, our lyricist, made these instruments and were replicas of the real thing, other than the one that played had a cassette player inside it!

A lot of props can be found at home, but if you need an old item like a large picture or large mirror with a moulded elaborate wooden frame, you will probably make the frame with wood and then use papier-mâché to create the fancy shapes. Papier-mâché is just wallpaper, past and recent newspaper, more or less, and based on pictures of fancy frame work.

When I put on 'Guys and Dolls' I wanted a coca cola sign that lit up inside. I wanted the sign to be 6'×4' in size so what I did was, buy a sheet of hardboard 6'x4' and a label from a coca cola bottle that was 4x6 inches.

I divided the 6'×4' hardboard into 3×3 inch squares and the 6x4 inch label into quarter of an inch squares like graph paper.

See drawing on next page

Enlarging a small picture into a large picture using a graph technique

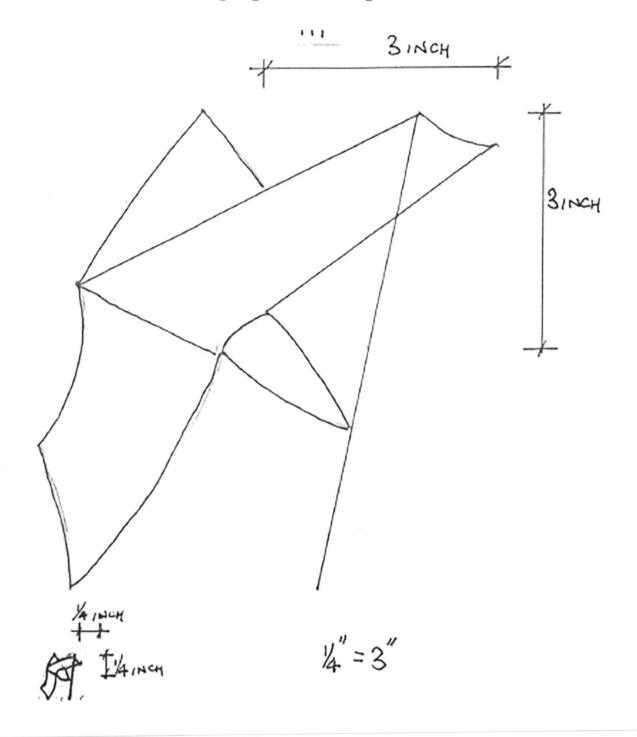

3 INCH

3 INCH

¼ INCH

1¼ INCH

¼" = 3"

Special Effects

Puppets

One year in Waltham Forest, the 'Bubble Theatre' came and set up their huge tent and put on 'Little Shop of Horrors', and I was asked if I would do a workshop for youngsters, which I did, (it was in the summer holidays) so I did various sketches, exercises etc. and one of the acts was a puppet show. Now, the Bubble Theatre are excellent and they have all the equipment and put on brilliant shows, and what they had was several curtain tracks, so what I did was buy some half inch wide white elastic, and found Sandie Shaw's music *Puppet on a String*. I was using six youngsters in the act so I cut up 24 lengths of elastic and tied them to one of the curtain tracks, and the other ends to the group's ankles and wrists.

We made up a dance and they all became puppets. At the end of the act, they all untied the elastic and let go as arranged and the stage crew were to clear the elastic strips. I'd already told one of the crew how to do it but somehow, they forgot and when I went behind the curtains, there was a six member stage crew looking up at the dangling elastic wondering how they could untie them! They were about 10 feet out of reach. So, without them knowing I went into the wings, pulled a string and all the strips fell to the stage. The crew couldn't stop laughing!

If you were to do a puppet act like this (it's great fun) it does require good choreography and then it will look great.

What you need is a wire rope across the stage (under tension) using strainers. Tie the elastic to the wire, pass a string through each knot and tie to the last elastic knot.

When you have to clear the dangling strips after the act, just pull the string and they will all gather up and end up at the side of the stage in the wings. You can untie the elastic when you want to.

See Drawing "A"

112

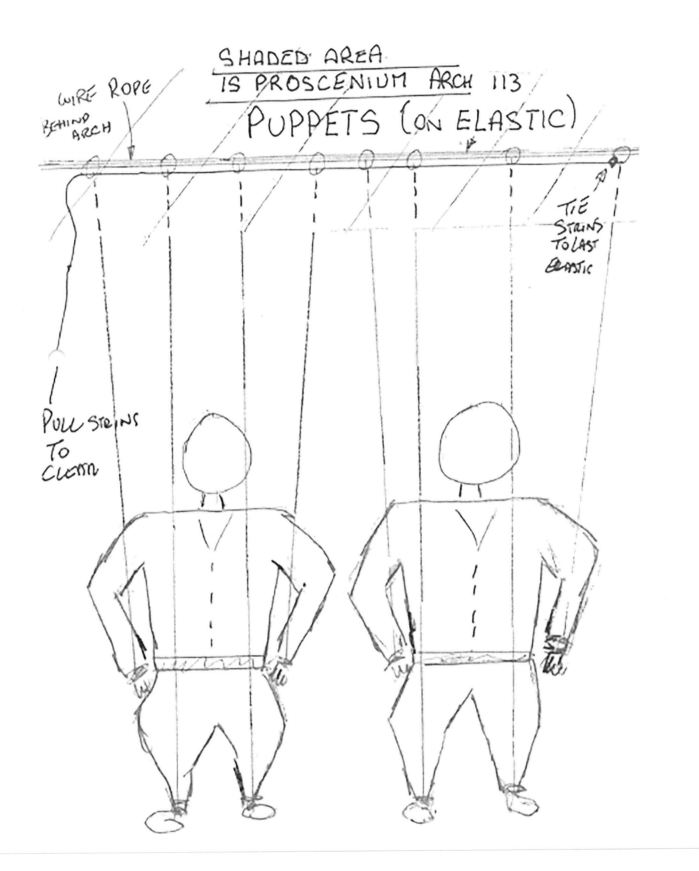

DRAWING 'A'

Special Effects

Scenery

When buying paints and curtains etc. always be aware of fireproofing. As I mentioned under 'venues' page 46, I built a mezzanine floor above the bar and across the rear wall of the centre. I used the correct steel channels and painted them with black matt emulsion, I cladded the front with tongue and groove and asked the fire brigade to check what I had built regarding fire prevention.

When the fire brigade inspected the structure, they said it wouldn't pass due to the tongue and groove cladding. Luckily, I told them I was going to paint the tongue and groove with flat black emulsion paint and they said, "That's fine, we thought you were going to varnish it." But with that in mind, always check what you're using and make sure the fire brigade checks things before you go too far.

There is a paint company called Bristol paints, if you google them and get information and prices, and then google theatrical suppliers and get prices for blackout paint, you can compare prices.

Blackout paint is about £18 per litre and when diluted, will cover around 200 sq. ft. (10 feet × 20 feet).

Blackout curtains, front tabs and gauzes are already treated for fire proofing. The best company I know is J.D.M.C Dougal Ltd. They have been established for 100 years and are very helpful. All curtains are made to order and can have ties at the top of the curtains, rings, hooks etc.

The bottom of the curtains can have a pocket that will take a conduit pipe if you want to have a large gauze curtain and you want to keep it taut, or you can use the pocket for a chain, mc Dougal's supply chains.

When using a gauze, the idea is you can paint a scene onto it which the audience will see. And the reason they will see it is because the gauze is lit from above and possibly the sides, across and in front of the gauze. This angle of lighting picks up the paint pigment.

If you were to light the gauze directly from the front, the light would go through the curtain and you would see most of what's behind the curtain. So we light the gauze properly and see the scene painted onto it. When you want the scene to disappear, you bring up lights behind the gauze and take out the gauze lights, a magical effect.

What you can do is paint invisible UV paint onto the gauze (in a darkish scene such as a cave), project light behind the gauze so as you can see behind dimly to give it atmosphere, and you can take out the dim lights, turn on a UV light and make the gauze an Aladdin's cave type scene or spiders web, etc.

Gauze is good in front of a picture frame painted, with let's say, your face, you sit behind the gauze in the same position as the painted gauze face, switch the lights and you become alive.

A really good effect is to have a scene on stage and behind a wall that is gauze, there is a scene in a room, ideally raised up on a rostra, when you do the light switch over, magic.

Don't forget blackout paint is very useful. You can paint invisible UV paint onto any scenery to transform the whole scene. Experiment all the time and you will come up with some brilliant ideas.

If you use ordinary UV paint instead of invisible UV paint, you can pick out various parts of the scene that you want to turn into something else when required. (You can Google uvgear.co.uk)

Dry ice is used to create an atmosphere. It sets the scene of a spooky or misty type of scene. It can be used off the ground to create a mist falling like a waterfall.

Dry ice, easy to obtain, it comes in blocks or pellets. Blocks seem to last longer than pellets, so ask for the blocks to be cut into smaller slabs. Before you use dry ice, which has to go into a dry ice machine, compare the effect with a smoke machine which is easier to use. Compare prices of buying a machine against hiring. These machines I am sure will be used many times, it may pay to buy.

When using smoke or dry ice, a very good effect is to close the front curtains, fill the stage with dry ice and when you open the curtains, the dry ice rolls off the stage into the audience.

I used this effect when I sang a song called 'The ghost of Benjamin Binns' a music hall song all about a ghost telling about his unfaithful wife. The scene was all black and in the middle of the stage was a 3ft high rostra. The ghost stands on the rostra throughout the song, and during the choruses, the ghost gets the audience to bang the floor with their feet; he doesn't tell them to do this, they automatically join in with him because of the music going 'bang bang'. The ghost is dressed in a very long white sheet that goes to the floor. Each chorus he waves his arms and stretches them outwards to the sides, like a cross. Each chorus, his arms extend a little more until the final chorus, they are both 6ft long.

To achieve this effect, you have two cardboard tubes each about 4ft long with white draped sleeves attached to them. Each chorus you let the tubes out a bit more. On the end of the tubes, you fit two mannequin hands with white gloves on them. Great fun.

Bangs, Etc

To create a scene like old London streets at night with a beam of light going through the smoke, you use smoke pellets. These are small tablet shaped pellets like peppermints. You light one of them with a match and it gives off smoke. This lingers in the air and gives a fantastic effect.

To create an old neglected room; dusty and cobwebby, use cobweb spray, this comes in aerosol cans. Also, you can buy fine cobweb material, then use clever back lighting.

If you need a loud bang, to make it more realistic than on the sound equipment, you use maroons. Maroons come in different sizes and are electrically set off. They can be battery operated but make sure you have a safety procedure in place. Nowadays they are operated electrically from control boxes with lights like, red = off, orange = get ready, green = go. This may be different coding but that's the basic idea, but it still comes down to a person to push the button. Practice your procedure carefully. The maroons are placed in a metal container with a mesh lid for safety.

If you have a scene with an old-fashioned camera that uses a flash, you use a flash pot, this creates a flash and smoke cloud. Basically, a container with flash powder in it and two wires coming from it which attaches to a battery. When you want it to go off, you already have one wire attached to the battery, you just have to touch the other wire to the other terminal. Obviously with total safety in mind.

Apple Dropping

When I produced the pantomime 'Old Mother Hubbard', I created a situation for 'Oh yes you are, oh no you're not'. The set for this consisted of an enormous tree (down stage left) on the corner of the stage, an Oak tree, its branches extended out and above the audience (as the audience plan shows Sheet C) and across the stage. This was a permanent fixture throughout the pantomime.

In the second half, Mother Hubbard has a scene where she's talking to the audience. "You see this tree boys and girls, and you big ones, well it's a truth tree." (Someone at the back of the audience shouts) "Oh no, it's not." (Mother Hubbard) "Oh yes, it is." This goes on for some time. "Anyway", she says, "if you are under this tree and you tell a lie, an apple will fall on your head." (Audience) "Oh no, it won't" etc. "Now, listen," Mother Hubbard says, "do you know the one thing that I never do? Guess what it is!" (Lots of banter with the audience) "No," she says, "I NEVER tell a lie," and an apple falls on her head. Obviously, she has to stand on the correct spot on the stage. This happens three times, three different lies, three different spots, on the stage.

She then picks a youngster on the carpet (where she knows the apples will drop) in front of the stage and says, "Do you tell fibs?" "No." "Do you always do what you're told?" If they say yes, an apple drops on their head. (The person operating the dropping of the apples needs to know when to do it. Probably the best way is for Mother Hubbard to put both hands on hips as the cue. You need to practice what method you will use.) "What about you, sir?" To someone in the audience, "Do you tell the wife how much money you've got?" Whatever he says, an apple drops on his head, if a woman is in the dedicated chair it won't matter, ask if she knows how much he's got.

"Now, boys and girls, are you all good boys and girls?" (You'll have to play this by ear) "YES" etc. on the third time, 10 apples fall onto the carpet area.

"Now, Mums and Dads," after lots of banter, and after the third YES and NO sequence, 30 apples fall onto the audience.

Mechanics Of Dropping Apples

On the 'mechanism drawing to drop an apple' (drawing A) the nail blocks are fixed to the tree branches and anywhere else where possible. The nails run through staples, these could be screw eyes which are better. The strings make their way (using screw eyes where needed) to the 'central string area' sheet B.

Before every show, the apples, (green polystyrene balls with cotton pushed through with a loop on the end to go onto the nail) have to be set up.

When the apples are being attached, the person that pulls the string has to ensure the strings are OK. (Two-person job)

When the apple-releasing person pulls the strings for apples 6 or 7, they grip all strings at the same time for 6 it's 'x1' and 7 it's 'x2'.

Make sure the strings are not too close to the wall when you build this system. You need to grasp them, or have a clamp that holds them all.

'A' and 'B' drilled wood (thin ply) must be fixed solidly to the wall, any movement could release the apples, there's only about an inch of nail holding the apple cotton on the blocks. (This needs practice, it's only a slight pull.)

Try and save all equipment from this effect for the future.

All blocks

Screw eyes

Strings

Drilled wood

When running strings from blocks to 'string operating area', ensure smooth running of string. No sharp bends. Instead of running each string individually from each block, you may want to design a way of joining strings together from one block to another. Personally, I preferred to use one string per block; it's far more reliable and less chance of strings snagging.

You can buy green polystyrene balls. Google it.

Mechanism to drop an apple

Drawing 'A'

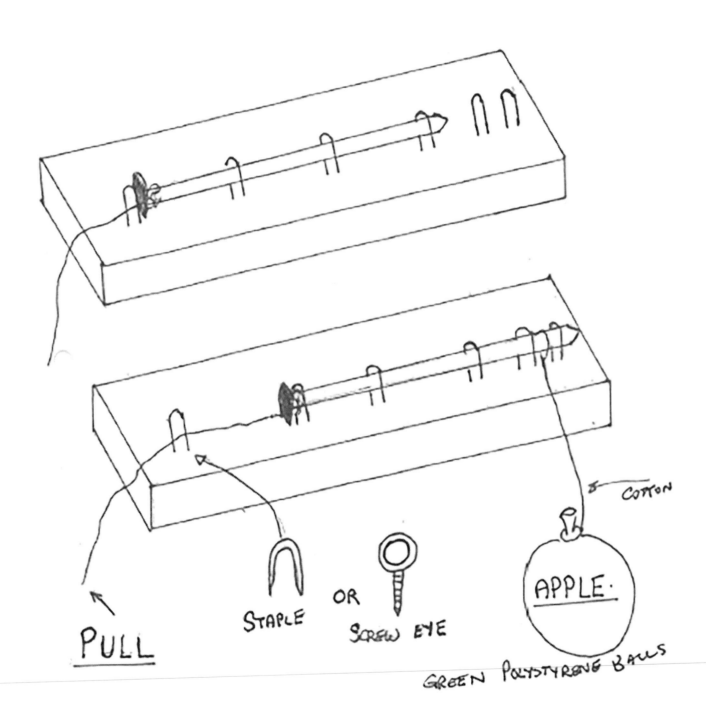

PULL

STAPLE

OR

SCREW EYE

APPLE·

COTTON

GREEN POLYSTYRENE BALLS

Tree Branches
Into the Audience and
Carpet

Sheet 'C'

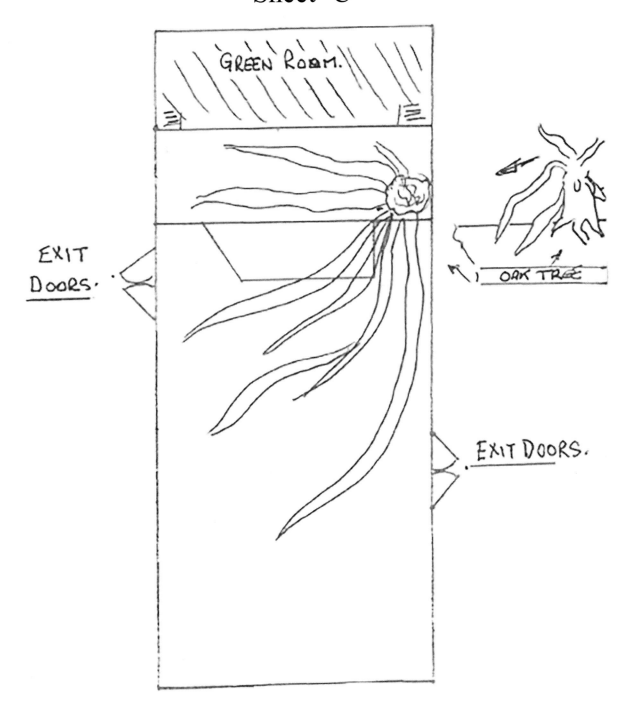

GREEN ROOM.

EXIT
DOORS.

OAK TREE

EXIT DOORS.

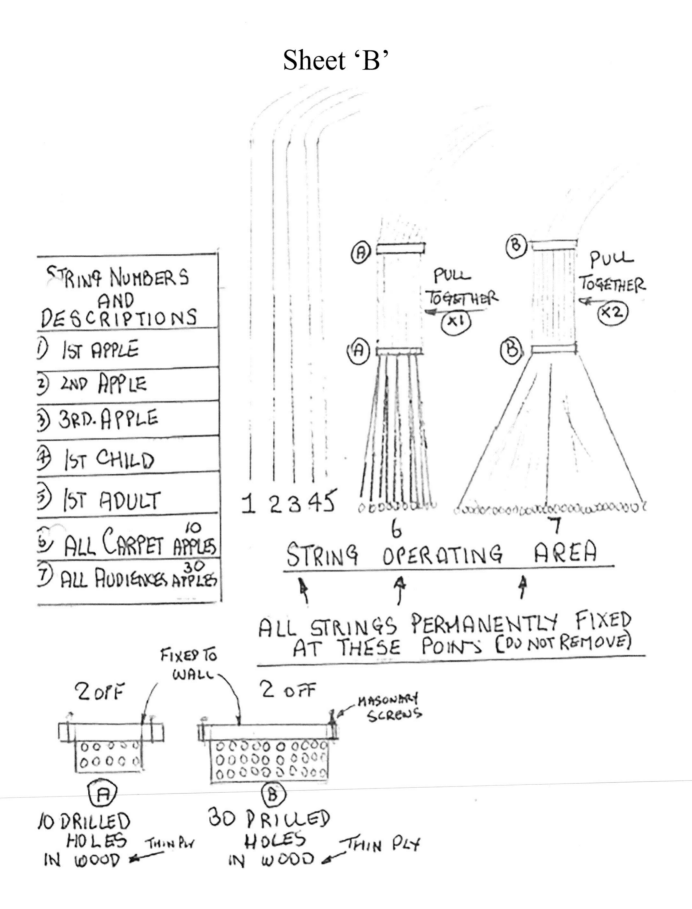

STRING NUMBERS AND DESCRIPTIONS

1) 1ST APPLE
2) 2ND APPLE
3) 3RD. APPLE
4) 1ST CHILD
5) 1ST ADULT
6) ALL CARPET APPLES 10
7) ALL AUDIENCES APPLES 30

1 2 3 4 5

PULL TOGETHER (X1)

PULL TOGETHER (X2)

6   7

STRING OPERATING AREA

ALL STRINGS PERMANENTLY FIXED
AT THESE POINTS (DO NOT REMOVE)

FIXED TO WALL

2 OFF   2 OFF

MASONARY SCREWS

(A)   (B)

10 DRILLED HOLES IN WOOD   THIN PLY

30 DRILLED HOLES IN WOOD   THIN PLY

Arrows Appearing

Basic Idea: Pantomime   'Robin Hood and the Wicked Squire'

During the play, villagers are worried because they haven't seen Robin Hood for a long time, when suddenly, the sound of a hunting horn is heard and a whistling arrow and then a loud thud. On a raised area on stage, a group of villagers have been standing and on the *thud* sound, they part in the middle and react to the fact that an arrow has landed in between them all. Robin appears.

Later in the play, the Squire challenges Robin Hood to an archery competition (for some reason) to see who can fire 5 arrows the quickest into a tree stage right.

The Squire goes 1st	Sound of whirling arrow and a crash of glass.	
Robin fires	1st arrow into the tree	
Squire	2nd arrow whirling sound a cow moos	
Robin	2nd arrow into tree.	
You get the idea.	5 arrows each	Let your imagination run wild!

How Do We Do It?

The 1 St arrow that lands between a group of villagers, see sheet '2' appeared on a sturdy flat 'B'

You need to fix a pipe onto the back of the flat which will house the arrow. You need to find a way of fixing this tube, obviously the flat gas to be very strong.

The arrow is set at the beginning of the show and the quiver needs to be masked. (Perhaps a leaf).

Obviously, the villagers have to stand in the correct positions for when the arrow is pushed through the flat from behind.

Practice, Practice. Practice.

The pushing of the arrow must be quick. Work out the stop on the arrow. It must be able to take a hammering!

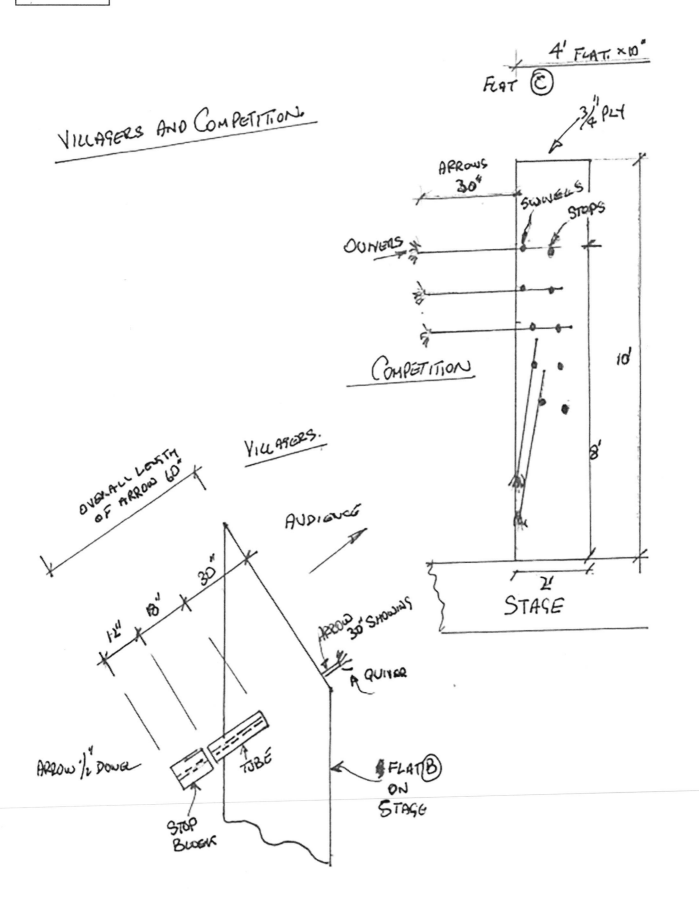

VILLAGERS AND COMPETITION.

4' FLAT. ×10"

FLAT C

3/4" PLY

ARROWS 30"

SWIVELS

STOPS

OWNERS

COMPETITION

10'

8'

2'

STAGE

OVERALL LENGTH OF ARROW 60"

VILLAGERS.

AUDIENCE

30"

18"

12"

ARROW 30' SHOWING

A QUIVER

ARROW 1/2" DOWEL

TUBE

STOP BLOCK

FLAT B ON STAGE

123

The Arrow Competition

Sheet 1 gives a detailed drawing of the mechanism to make arrows appear to stick in a tree on stage.

You need a sturdy method for the 'swivel point'. Taking care with the holes for the bolts, they take a lot of pressure. I recommend half-inch diameter bolts.

When I did this some years back, I used plywood and put the mechanisms on it which made it easier to lay out and see what I was doing. So you end up with a strip of ply say 8 feet × 18 inches with all the workings on it and all you have to do is fix it to the flat.

You need 2x2 timber to fix the arrows to so that it is robust.

You will have to work out the stops which is where the arrows 2x2 timber stops after you execute the move. These take a hammering.
And the 2x2 timber has to be fixed to the stop somehow most of this is worked out as you go.

Hopefully you can understand sheet 'T' but basically you pull down on the 2x2 timber as hard as possible onto the stops. This will make the arrows shudder.

How do we get rid of the arrows from the squires and robins bows?

They will be aiming their arrows from stage left to stage right.

They hold their bow in their left hand
And appear to put the arrow onto the string with their right.
In fact, they hold the string next to the arrow not in a slot.
(This will require practice.)

A person, masked by the scenery, stands on the right of the archer and behind them.

As the archer holds the arrow and pulls the string back the person behind puts their right hand over the arrow (palm facing downwards) and gets a hold of the arrow.

On the cue, they jerk their right hand from the wrist and remove the arrow. As the arrow is removed the archer lets go of the string (at the same time).
This whole sequence requires a lot of practice; both with the movements and the sound effects.

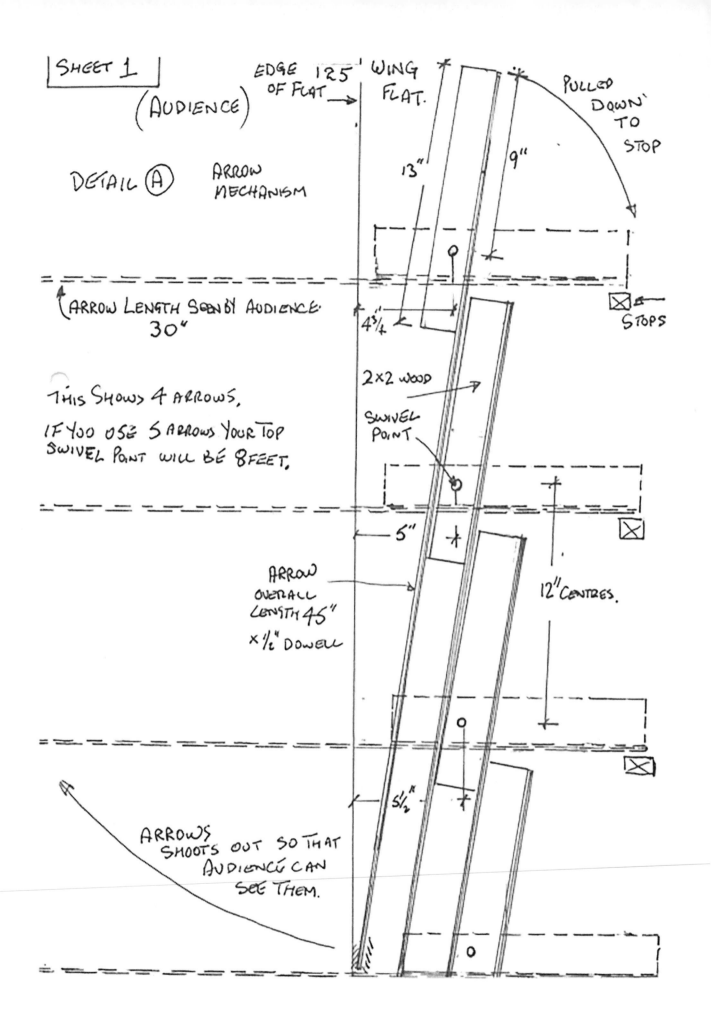

SHEET 1

(AUDIENCE)

DETAIL Ⓐ   ARROW MECHANISM

EDGE OF FLAT → 125' WING FLAT.

13"   9"   PULLED DOWN TO STOP

Stops

↑ ARROW LENGTH SEEN BY AUDIENCE. 30"

4¾"

2×2 WOOD

SWIVEL POINT

THIS SHOWS 4 ARROWS.

IF YOU USE 5 ARROWS YOUR TOP SWIVEL POINT WILL BE 8 FEET.

5"

12" CENTRES.

ARROW OVERALL LENGTH 45" × ½" DOWELL

5½"

ARROWS SHOOTS OUT SO THAT AUDIENCE CAN SEE THEM.

Floating Ghost Lantern

Basic Idea: Pantomime   'Goldilocks and the Haunted Castle'

A scared person creeps across the stage, followed by a floating lantern 6 feet off the ground with a lit candle in it. The scared person exits at stage right followed by the lantern.

After 3 seconds, the scared person comes back on from stage right followed by the lantern and both exit stage left.

This is an impressive effect and can be used many times in the show and you could put a white calico sheet attached to the lantern like a ghost.

Another effect that can be achieved but would require you designing the effect on site is:

A person comes onto stage backwards from stage left and another person comes on backwards from stage right. The lantern is in the centre of the stage, as the two people get close to the lantern. It rises up and stops above their heads. They don't see one another and when in the middle (under the lantern) they both pass each other, turn around and start to go off. The lantern comes back down and follows one of them off.

(I will describe at the end how to do above effect.)

Mechanics of a Floating Lantern.

Look at detailed instructions sheet.

'FLOATING GHOST LANTERN'

Note! Before reading instructions look at 'Floating Ghost Instructions' to get the gist of it first.

1. Fix eye shield anchors to both walls 'X'.

2. Wire rope. 3/16 thick. '2a' make a loop '3a' one end using wire rope clamps '4a'. Put 40 oval shape rings '5a' onto wire rope. Get correct length for rope and make another loop. (Allowing for the strainers.)

3. Put the strainers onto the ends of the wire rope and put onto the eye shield anchors. Tighten the wire rope to a good tension. Put 20 rings each side of the wire rope.

4. Fix with ordinary raw plugs a screw eye 'd1' under the eye shield anchors at 'xx'.

5. Two 26-foot lengths of string t and '2' tie both strings to the centre ring '4'.

   You now have to fix the strings to the oval rings, as in the diagram of ring '4' at one-foot spaces which is not easy. You may know a way of doing this quickly. The only way I know is to make a loop every foot and then tie with string the loop to the ring.

   (The reason for the rings is to support the string 'a' which pulls the lantern '6a'.)

6. Once the rings are attached, move the centre ring '4' to stage right or as you are looking at the drawing you left. Then tie string t to the eye shield anchor stage left or your right as you are looking.

   Now move centre ring '4' to stage left, your right, and tie string '2' to stage right your left, to eye shield anchor at stage right your left.

   You will notice the string gathers as shown at '5'.

7. Two more 26-foot lengths of string 'a' and 'b.' tie string 'b' to centre ring '4' and pass the string through the rings to stage left and through screw eye 'di' at 'xx'. Then tie string 'a' to centre ring '4' and pass the string through the rings to stage right and through screw eye 'df' at 'xx'.

8. Now tie the lantern '6a' to the centre ring '4' to the required length the lantern can have a battery-operated candle fixed inside. The string that ties onto the lantern has to be very thin. You can use magician's wire. Google it. You don't want the audience to see it. Thin wire as shown at 'ff'.

9. Now practice and see the lantern move by pulling strings 'a' and 'b'

As mentioned above; there is another effect you can work out but will require some thought so let's give you the idea.

Screw an ordinary screw eye, stage centre, above the wire that you have put in, perhaps in a joist or something.

Pass a string through it and tie it to the lantern. The string to the linter needs to be about 4 feet of special wire (Invisible) as 'ff'.

Using screw eyes, get the string to a wing area.

You can now lift the lantern upwards and out of sight.

Let's put two strings to the lantern so it can be operated from both sides of the stage. This is like puppeteers that use poles with items hanging by an invisible wire operated from the wings.

You now need to play. This could be a brilliant effect, Good Luck.

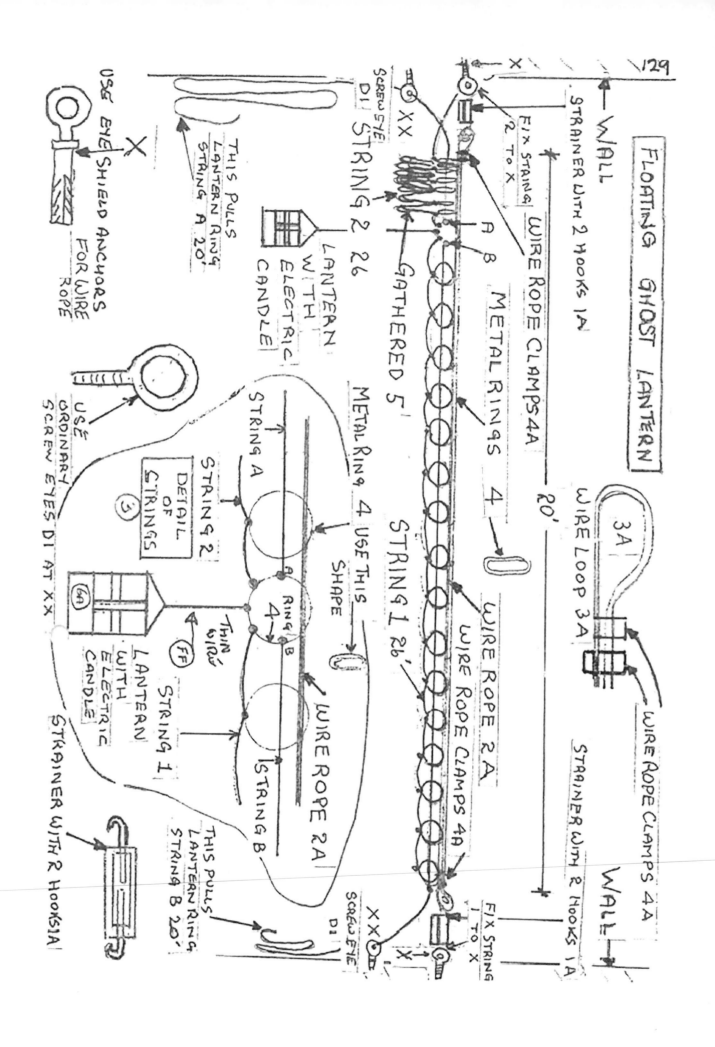

FLOATING GHOST LANTERN

STRAINER WITH 2 HOOKS 1A

WALL

WIRE ROPE CLAMPS 4A

3A

WIRE LOOP 3A

STRAINER WITH 2 HOOKS 1A

WALL

WIRE ROPE CLAMPS 4A

FIX STRING 2 TO X

SCREW EYE D1

STRING 2 26

GATHERED 5'

METAL RINGS 4A

METAL RINGS 4

20'

WIRE ROPE CLAMPS 4A

WIRE ROPE 2A

THIS PULLS LANTERN RING STRING A 20'

LANTERN WITH ELECTRIC CANDLE

USE EYE SHIELD ANCHORS FOR WIRE ROPE

USE ORDINARY SCREW EYES D1 AT XX

STRING A

STRING 2

DETAIL OF STRINGS

Ring 4

A

B

Thin Wire

FF

LANTERN WITH ELECTRIC CANDLE

STRING 1

METAL RING 4 USE THIS SHAPE

STRING 1 26

1 STRING B

WIRE ROPE 2A

SCREW EYE

XX

6A

FIX STRING 1 TO X

XX

SCREW EYE

THIS PULLS LANTERN RING STRING B 20'

D1

STRAINER WITH 2 HOOKS 1A

Paul Daniels

A Magical Time

I put on a musical called 'Jack The Ripper'. The scenes take place on the streets of old London and in a Victorian music hall. In one of the music halls acts, a magician, makes a woman appeared from a box with her throat cut (one of the ripper's victims).

The script suggested a large cubicle is brought on with the victim concealed inside, this seemed impossible with our restricted stage space and I discussed it with the group. Gerry, one of the girls said, "I'll ask Paul."

"Who's Paul?" I said.

"Paul Daniels, he's a friend." She said she would get in touch with him.

Paul Daniels at the time was one of the world's top magicians. His TV show 'The Paul Daniels Magic Show' ran on the BBC from 1979–1994.

Anyway, rehearsals went on and about 3 weeks later on a Sunday morning we were rehearsing, who comes into the centre, Paul Daniels. "Hello, Chris. I'm Paul, Gerry's friend. Can I watch some of your rehearsal?"

"Of course, you can, pull up a chair."

After about 15 minutes he came up to me and said, "Right, Chris, can I show you my idea on someone appearing on stage?" He went to his car, came back and went into the wings. He then came on stage, introduced himself as a magician and began a magician's act.

He came out with flat folded thin plywood painted like a Wendy house and started placing these pieces of wood (no taller than 30 inches high) and eventually built a small Wendy house with a roof, the lot.

He then said 'and now may I present, Gerry!' The Wendy house collapsed and up jumped Gerry! I'd love to tell you how this was done but I daren't.

With that, I got to talking with Paul and he asked, "Are these your stage lights?"

"No," I said, "as it happens, these are other groups' light but they unexpectedly need them back, we've got a bit of a problem but we'll get around it somehow."

Paul stayed for a while watching the rehearsal then came up to me and said, "Chris, I'm going home but I'll be back."

And off he went. I honestly thought to myself, I don't think he'll be back, but two hours later in came Paul, "Give us a hand lad." And in came 12 cardboard boxes. Twelve brand new stage lights. So we took him to our regular Indian restaurant where he entertained the customers and staff, what a fella!

About a year later a friend and I, a fellow actor, were trying to get a theatre built in Waltham Forest, my friend, Phill was an architect, and we were at the point where we could do with a well-known person to become a patron of the theatre.

With that, Gerry once again stepped up, and within weeks drives up to my house in a Rolls Royce with his wife Debbie, Paul Daniels.

They were asked around for dinner and came along. We had a great night; lots of magical fun, jokes and stories. They were both wonderful people and so was Gerry who was at the meal. That's how things happen!

The Cottage

Obviously, there are the outdoor theatres. Usually, these are in places where a stage can be erected or a natural shape in the ground similar to an amphitheatre. We used to do shows in abridge Essex that had such a shape.

Dick Williams, who taught me theatre when I first started in drama, had a cottage in Abridge way off the road in the forest. Quite close to the cottage was an old rubbish tip. One day Dick and his son David decided to get rid of all the rubbish. It turned out that the tip was in a natural hole in the ground. To cut a very long story short, they ended up with an outdoor theatre the shape of an amphitheatre.

The audience sat on cut out steps about 30ft high facing the stage which had a backcloth of high trees and bushes. This venue brings so many memories back to so many people.

Theatrical lights and music in the forest.

Entrances and exits through the woods to the dressing rooms.

And all performances on a grass stage looking up at all those people in the audience.

It sat around 200–300. On a warm summer's night. Sheer magic!

We don't mention the rain and gnats!

I'll always remember in a music hall, we put on an old acrobatic act. After much activity we came to our last final spectacle. We had a big cannon and an almighty bang with clouds of smoke and suddenly through the smoke a dummy shot out towards the audience it went up above their heads and into the trees. It was a life size dummy and at the end of the show as we took our bow the dummy came back over the audience's heads for its bow. Those were the days.

The Minack Theatre

The Minack Theatre is an amphitheatre in Cornwall on the cliffs at Porthcurno.

Rowen cade from a young girl to her eighties, built it by hand at a spot on the cliffs at the end of her garden, she died just before her ninetieth birthday. The 1st show was put on in 1932 'the tempest'. In 1962, 'the tempest' was put on for the theatres 60th anniversary in which I played a drunken sailor, I needed hardly any rehearsals!

The theatre is out of this world and definitely worth a visit. It seats 700 people and the backcloth is the sea, with sightings of dolphins a regular occurrence.

The group were asked to do the production because of their reputation, I was asked to be in the production by the director who was a friend of mine. The group mainly produced Shakespeare plays and were very talented and built good sets. They were building the mast of the ship that gets wrecked and were having a bit of trouble as the mast had to break in two and was very heavy, they really were making a proper mast, all wood.

Could see time was running out so I said to one of the guys, come on let's go to town. We found a carpet shop and they kindly gave us several large cardboard tubes that the carpets came on. Back we went and weren't they pleased. 'Why didn't we think of that,' then, everything was okay?

You can take good money at the Minack and it is very popular both with the audience and theatre companies that appear there. You need to pick the right production to fit the unique setting. It seems strange that some companies put on plays that take place in a room. Maybe they are more interested in making money than producing a production that gives you a ready-made atmospheric advantage that allows you to pull at the heartstrings of the audience. They should really put on Mamma Mia! But this is a venue to help finance your own organisations and have a really enjoyable experience.

Stage Lighting

Lanterns and their use

Flood lights	One main use for floodlights is to light the back wall of the stage, you can't really control the spread of flood lights. Most stages you will see long light boxes on the back wall high up. These are boxes with Individual compartments with coloured bulbs in them or coloured gels. If you were to put a flood light in front of the stage it will take out most features of an actor's face.
Follow spot	Mostly used to follow an actor around the stage, as in singers etc. They're very powerful and useful in other ways such as picking out various areas on the stage.
Lanterns/Fresnel's	Some lights have facilities built in to their design to be able to do various things such as:
A. Gobos	A piece of thin sheet metal that you can cut out a design. This can be placed into the lantern and when turned on will display the design onto the wall or scenery. A typical design would be forked lightning.
B. Shutters	Using sutures allows you to project squares or rectangles etc. As an example, if you have a picture on a wall which is oblong in shape, with shutters you are able to light exactly the same shape as the picture frame. Or, if you need to light the scenery at the corner of the proscenium arch you can cut out, with shutters, the arch with a straight line of light.
C Irisis	An iris allows you to make a circular spot larger or smaller.
D GELLS	Coloured filters and gels, come in rolls or sheets and can be cut to any size and fits on the front of a lantern in a frame to give colour. And can be used for various effects.
Strobe	Gives a pulsating light ideal for an old-fashioned film scene. It slows things down. If ever used in a theatre, the audience must be aware as it can cause distress.

| UV lights | You can just use a UV tube it's cheaper. UV lighting is Used in conjunction with UV paint effects. |
| Modern Lights | There are so many sophisticated lights on the market; your best bet is get in touch with strand lighting and enquire about their lighting workshops. |

Lighting uses.

1. To help see the facial features. If you light only from the front you will flatten a person's facial features.

2. Side lights and down lights give character/shadows to the face. Makes them more interesting.

3. Back lighting enhances the actors head, shoulders etc. Experiment.

4. Full back lighting with a strong light such as a follow spot will give a special effect to a person. Try it!

5. Sometimes less lighting is better. There's no need to flood the stage.

6. Try dimming the lights and experiment, see what affects you can achieve.

7. I remember once I built a huge 4' daffodil and fixed it in front of the proscenium arch above the stage. The show was to do with a garden called 'the plotters of cabbage patch corner'. For some reason I put fairy lights behind the daffodil's petals. When I turned the lights on, *what an effect!* It became 3D. You must experiment! Like putting a spot light in a treasure chest in a dim cave, with coloured gels so when the lid of the chest is lifted the light shines out onto the actor's faces and upwards. Wham!

Curtains

Curtains for Masking	You can't have too many blackout curtains. They can conceal the next scene. They can create a black stage and let the audience imagine the setting that you are portraying. They can mask entrances and exits and they can cover objects. Just get lots.
Front Tabs	The front curtains are so important regarding the feeling of the forthcoming scene/event.

Slow Opening Curtain Slow Closing Curtain	Sad	Worried	Quiet Scene
Fast Opening Curtain Fast Closing Curtain	Happy	Exciting	Surprise

Curtains must be rehearsed

Draped Curtains

The other way to use the front curtains is to drape them.

As detail C1 shows on page 1.

The actions are the same as front curtain details (sad, happy etc.)

Most front curtains are gathered at the top which helps the draping.

When sewing the rings to the curtains, for the ropes to run through, make sure you not only sew to the lining, but also to the curtain. Being very careful.

You may have to experiment where the rings have to be sewn to give a drape shape that you like.

This effect is ideal for singers or solo acts to come through.

The drape can then drop after their entrance and open and close on their exit.

All curtains must be practiced.

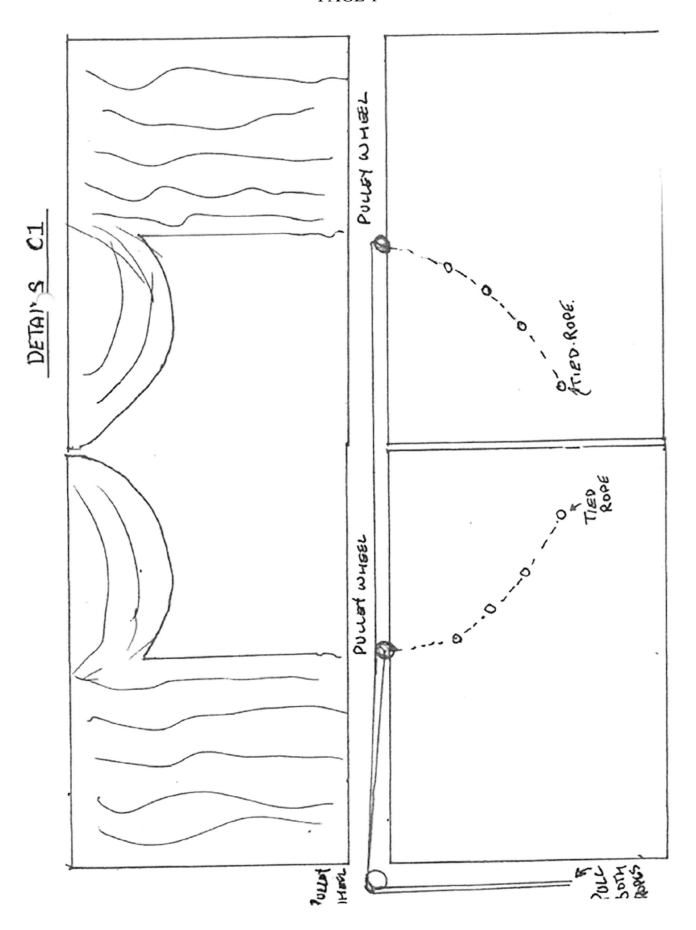

DETAILS C1

PULLEY WHEEL

PULLEY WHEEL

PULLEY WHEEL

(TIED ROPE.

TIED ROPE

PULL BOTH ROPES.

Sound

When I used to put on 'music hall' on a regular basis, we always played Strauss music, mostly waltzes. Some of the cast said, "oh, not again." But over time it became a tradition and both cast and audience got used to it and became expected.

It gave an atmosphere to the proceedings.

'The players theatre' at Charing cross, Villiers street, always played certain music as the audience came in and began every show with the same songs at the start and the audience were expected to join in.

When choosing music to be played as the audience comes in and for the interval, it's important to set the mood for the show.

For 'Guys and Dolls', maybe New Orleans type of music.

'Grease' maybe small parts of music from that period.

Never put on music that competes with your show. Just snippets to get into the mood of the show.

'Dracula' Austrian style music (maybe).

This takes time but is very important.

You may find that you want to choose certain music or sounds that enhance the mood of the scenes in a play, or you may find that the person in charge of operating the sound has that ability, in which case, can be a joint process.

You will need access to plenty of music and sound effects. BBC sound affect recordings are excellent.

There may come a time when you have to make your own sound effect or adapt to ones that you have. This is where certain techniques are chosen to do this.

When I was producing, Gary, A brilliant sound engineer and a very good friend, used reel to reel which involved cutting and splicing. (Cutting the tape and joining it back).

This technique was used for shows, using reel to reel equipment. When you had to add sounds to a tape that was finished, you would record the sound onto a piece of tape, cut the finished tape at the spot where you wanted the sound to go, and join the sound tape to it, cut the new piece of tape and join it to the finished tape.

All sound cues were written on white tape and cut and spliced onto the main tape. Lots of fun.

When producing a musical, a very good technique that I used to use was at the end of a scene, play a very tiny bit of music from a song that will be sung latter. This sound stays in the audiences mind and when the song is sung, the brain remembers it. This really does work.

Many shows have the orchestra play parts of the show just before the curtain goes up, the 'overture'. Personally, I think this spoils the surprise of what's to come.

Volumes for the music and sound effects are decided by the director and levels are written down by the sound operator onto their cue sheets.

If music is written within the group, it is well worthwhile going to a sound recording studio and have the music orchestrated. Not only does it sound amazing, it's an amazing experience, you may need a musical director (MD) as previously mentioned.

Now Then.
Let's Imagine You've Read The Book.

If you are already involved in theatre, you may have got a couple of ideas from the book, but, you probably will do your own thing.

Good luck and may you put many productions on.

If you are not involved in theatre, but you've always wanted to be and you're enthusiastic, you've got patience and you can organise, then following this book will guide you, with help from friends, etc. in producing a venue. When established, this venue will give you lots of pleasure and a large achievement factor.

Now this is probably how most amateur groups end up and are really happy as I was for many years. But as we are in a very creative industry why don't we look at going further and see what we could achieve.

This next step is like writing a
Full Length 'Musical'

**The musical is called
'Imagine'**

**You have just read a book guiding you through
various aspects of the theatre.**

You now have your own venue, with all the facilities you require to put on productions.

You have an army of actors, trades people, helpers and contacts spanning many aspects of the theatre industry.

But you are still enthusiastic, you've proved you're patient and you can certainly organise.

Let's expand.

1st Project

Let's go to the local job centre and put an idea to them that might make you money and at the same time give people out of work something to aim at.

(You must earn money to finance this expansion)

The idea is, offer people out of work to come along to your theatre, get involved, get introduced to loads of trades and become more confident when looking for employment. You train them up and within 6 months, you put on a full-length musical all about being unemployed and being helped by a theatre, a bit like 'Grease'.

If the show is a success, you can see about the government sponsoring the idea to all job centres.

Trades	Personally
Carpentry	Confidence
Building a set	Conversation techniques
Scenery painting	Speaking up
Making props	Using the brain for ideas
Costume making	Helping people
Stage lighting	Working in a team
Sound operating	Working towards a show

And lots lots more.

Next theatre project

Build up several touring casts to make money: under the name of

'Imagine Theatre'

Murder weekends

Old time music halls

School shows T.I.E. (theatre in education)

Pantomimes

Shakespeare workshops

Hire large venues:

Minack theatre

Loads of outdoor theatres

The list is endless

Workshops for schools at your theatre. Introduce children to all aspects of the theatre ending in a short show for parents and teachers.

Next theatre project

At theatre or your premises nearby:

Scenery Manufacture	for hire or sell
Costume Making (and alterations)	for hire or sell
Back drops painted	at a price
Scenery Painting	at a price
Lighting	for hire or sell
Lighting Operator	at a price

And finally, at the centre

A dedicated group of writers:

Pantomimes

Musicals

Songwriters

Lyricists

Full time classes at theatre or close by:

Writing of plays	Tuition fees
Writing of pantomimes	Tuition fees
Technical drawing	Tuition fees
Stage lighting	Tuition fees
Sound recording	Tuition fees
Directing	Tuition fees
Costume design, manufacture	Tuition fees

Well, how was that?

If you put all the items together that have just been listed, you will have a major theatrical company in your hands.

'Imagine'

Good luck.

Don't say I didn't give you some ideas.

Chris.

Index

PAGE

PAGE

PAGE